H²h
How to Help

The Gifted Learner
How to Help

Fidelma Healy Eames

The Gifted Learner

© Pavilion Publishing & Media

The author has asserted her rights in accordance with the Copyright, Designs and Patents Act (1988) to be identified as the author of this work.

Published by:

Pavilion Publishing and Media Ltd
Blue Sky Offices, 25 Cecil Pashley Way
Shoreham by Sea, West Sussex
BN43 5FF

Tel: 01273 434 943
Email: info@pavpub.com
Web: www.pavpub.com

Published 2022

All rights reserved. No part of this publication may be reproduced, stored in a retrieval system, or transmitted in any form or by any means, electronic, mechanical, photocopying, recording or otherwise, without prior permission in writing of the publisher and the copyright owners.

A catalogue record for this book is available from the British Library.

ISBN: 978-1-80388-050-1

Pavilion Publishing and Media is a leading publisher of books, training materials and digital content in mental health, social care and allied fields. Pavilion and its imprints offer must-have knowledge and innovative learning solutions underpinned by sound research and professional values.

Author: Fidelma Healy Eames
Cover design: Emma Dawe, Pavilion Publishing and Media Ltd
Page layout and typesetting: Emma Dawe, Pavilion Publishing and Media Ltd
Printing: CMP

Contents

Series Preface v
About the Author vi
Author's Preface viii
How to Use This Book xiii

Part 1: Introduction 1
    Chapter 1: What is giftedness? 3
    Chapter 2: Why do gifted learners matter? 9
    Chapter 3: Models of giftedness 15
    Chapter 4: Testing and assessment 23
    Ten key things to know about giftedness and gifted learners 28

Part 2: Learning characteristics 29
    Chapter 5: Curiosity 31
    Chapter 6: Problem-solving 37
    Chapter 7: Avid reading 45
    Chapter 8: Quick learning 53

Part 3: Creativity 61
    Chapter 9: Cognitive flexibility 63
    Chapter 10: Language usage 67
    Chapter 11: Creativity and imaginative expression 73
    Chapter 12: Sense of humour 79

Part 4: Motivation and leadership 83
    Chapter 13: Motivation and task commitment 85
    Chapter 14: Boredom 91
    Chapter 15: Competitiveness 97
    Chapter 16: Leadership 105

Part 5: Social and emotional development 113
    Chapter 17: Self-esteem and acceptance 115
    Chapter 18: Perfectionism 121
    Chapter 19: Over-excitability and intensity 127
    Chapter 20: Stress and anxiety 131

Part 6: Inclusion and curriculum provision 139
    Chapter 21: Underachieving gifted learners **141**
    Chapter 22: The twice-exceptional (2e) learner **147**
    Chapter 23: Curriculum differentiation **153**
    Chapter 24: Best practice to support gifted learners **161**

Part 7: Conclusion 167
    Chapter 25: Summary **169**
    Chapter 26: A last word to parents and carers **177**
    Chapter 27: A last word to teachers and schools **179**

Index of *How to Help* advice **181**
Appendices **183**
References **207**

Series Preface

Young people in today's society face considerable stresses. The Prince's Trust, which has monitored youth opinion for ten years, found that just under half of young people who use social media now feel more anxious about their future when they compare themselves to others on websites and apps such as Instagram, Twitter and Facebook. A similar proportion agreed that social media makes them feel 'inadequate'. The *Guardian Weekly* noted in early 2019 that more than half of young people think that social media creates 'overwhelming pressure' to succeed.

There are many issues that are likely to affect every pupil at some point during his or her time at school. How these are dealt with can be 'make or break' for some pupils, because of the crucial stages in education that can be affected. The implications are deep and broad because, understandably, the child's experience of education, and his or her success at school, can have a tremendous impact on later life chances.

The *How to Help* series covers a broad and comprehensive range of topics that will have resonance for today's parents, carers and educators. Each title is designed to make a valuable contribution in the breadth of issues that it introduces, and the realistic helping strategies that it puts forward.

Gavin Reid and Jennie Guise
Series Editors

About the Author

Dr. Fidelma Healy Eames, PhD, MSc, BEd has a long background in teaching and learning and teacher education. She is Director and Lead Educator with Study & Careers (www.studyandcareers.ie), an education, wellbeing and careers consultancy based in Galway, Ireland. A former politician (Senator, Councillor and Education spokesperson in Seanad Éireann, 2004-2016), Fidelma maintains an active interest in education policy and public affairs and is a regular media contributor.

Growing up on a farm in Galway imbued Fidelma with a strong work ethic and sense of self, traits she has carried into her professional life. Her enduring interest is in making life and learning easier for students, teachers and parents at primary, second and further education levels. She is passionate about enabling learners to develop the mindset and skills for success, and rejoices in their taking 'ownership' of their own learning.

Her PhD research focused on language and learning and the learner's voice in writing. In 2002 she began offering 'learning to learn' and wellbeing courses to second-level schools and colleges across Ireland with a team of specially trained teachers. In 2006 she published *Switching on for Learning: A Student Guide to Exam & Career Success* which has become a core text for teachers, parents and students interested in enabling independent learning. In response to COVID-19, and to make remote learning easier for students, she developed a six-module online blended programme called *Switching on for Learning: Becoming an Independent Learner*[1].

More recently, Fidelma has expanded her consultancy services to include career guidance, coaching and personality profiling for students and adults in career transition. She is an accredited tester in the areas of ability, personality, occupational and emotional intelligence and educational assessment with the British Psychological Society. Excited about people's futures, her individual advice and support to young people and their families has been a catalyst for many to find their niche and forge a more fulfilling path. Her recent interview series for schools, *Inspiring Ireland Inspiring Students*, is testament to her interest in facilitating new ways to inspire young people[2].

As a teacher educator Fidelma supervises student placement with Hibernia College and is an advisor to the Confucius Institute at the

---

1 https://studyandcareers.ie/switching-on-for-learning/
2 https://studyandcareers.ie/inspiring-ireland/

National University of Ireland (NUI), Galway. Along with associates she offers a specialist course in Teacher Education Interview preparation for the Professional Masters' in Education (PME). An active collaborator, her research interests include language, literacy and learning across the spectrum, the writer's voice, wellbeing and issues relating to parents and the home-school environment.

Author's Preface

Welcome to this book on the gifted learner. It is part of the 'How to Help' series and I focus on that perspective throughout. The ultimate intention is for it to be a resource for educators, teachers, parents and caregivers of gifted learners, so that we may arrive at a greater plateau of awareness about how to help this unique cohort to achieve their potential.

Throughout my research for the book, it became clear that gifted learners are frequently under-served, largely because they are seen as bright and consequently capable of managing alone and without specialist support. This couldn't be further from the truth. Another common misconception is that gifted learners automatically excel in every area whereas, in reality, high ability in one area may coexist with a usual level of ability or a learning difficulty in other areas.

While acknowledging that gifted students are capable in many extraordinary ways, they can also be a vulnerable and frequently misunderstood cohort. They need and deserve to be recognised and seen for their differences, understood, and supported holistically at cognitive and affective levels. On one occasion I heard myself describing the gifted learner as 'seeing differently' and this may reflect how they interact with the world.

So how will this book help?

It is intended to be a comprehensive guide. Chapters are informed by the insights, experiences and advice of nineteen gifted learners, their parents, and also a nominated teacher in most cases.[3] This gives an authenticity, realness and depth to the book that I value greatly. Each chapter highlights research in the specific topic under discussion, includes supporting quotes from the case studies, and, importantly, presents a 'how to help' section for teachers and parents.

It is notable that the gifted learners I interviewed for this book span a wide age range from ten to fifty-eight years, representing learners from a wide range of educational levels. This is significant and deliberate. It is useful for teachers and parents to see the life path, the potential and the possibility for gifted learners, and it is heartening to hear their voices as they express their strengths and vulnerabilities, their successes and their disappointments. Each interview lasted approximately ninety minutes,

---

[3] A total of fifty-four interviews were carried out; details of those who took part can be found in Appendix 1.

addressing the interview question schedule designed for learner, teacher and parent respectively (see Appendices 6-8).

Throughout the process, I grew in awareness about the uniqueness of gifted learners and developed a healthy respect for their differences. I was amazed to hear how much they enjoyed the interview process in relation to their own lives, how they learned, how they interacted, and how they coped, survived and thrived. Fifteen-year-old **Ava**'s comment was not uncommon: *"I liked the gifted learner interview, it opened my eyes about everything, it's good to know there are other people like me."* Because gifted learners feel different and are different, the desire to know that there are others like them is significant.

Giftedness, described as *"a blessing and a curse"* by **Ruby**'s mother, sets the challenge and the trajectory for this book. At the outset I want to thank you for joining me on this journey of discovery about gifted learning, and for being open to the sound and exciting reasons for us to invest in our gifted learners. I hope that this book will help you to unlock their potential, and to support them so that their gift may become a talent that is realised, seen and celebrated in practice, to enrich their own life and the lives of others.

Praise for this book

"This timely book on gifted children is a much-needed resource for a very under-researched group. It contains important, relevant and helpful information for teachers, parents and anyone working with gifted children. Much of the previous literature in this field focuses on gifted children as a homogeneous group, and I am delighted that this book reflects the diversity and differences within this population and suggests effective and practical ways of working with these different groups. It also recognises that the social and emotional needs of gifted children are as important as their academic needs, and highlights best practice to deal with these issues."
Dr Colm O'Reilly
Director, Centre for Talented Youth, Ireland
Dublin City University

"This book is a must read for anyone that supports the gifted and talented population. Fidelma Healy Eames imagines a world where each unique gifted learner is seen, heard and wholly understood. She discusses an individual's strengths, vulnerabilities and motivations providing a framework for parents, caregivers, clinicians and educators to identify gifted learners and to immediately build individualised intervention plans to fully support their development. Seeing gifted learners through Healy Eames's eyes may be the pivotal moment that changes the future outcomes of your gifted learners."
Corinne Cooper, Illinois, USA
Parent of twice-exceptional child

"This timely and essential book provides an authoritative overview on key aspects of giftedness for which there is such a need. The case studies bring key aspects of the research to life and provide a basis for clear and comprehensive guidelines, supported by appropriate strategies to improve the approach of classroom educators and their families. It is user friendly, accessible and should be read by all educators and parents interested in gifted learners. I'm excited for the difference it can make to learners' lives and their educational experience."
Dr Sandra Ryan
Mary Immaculate College
University of Limerick, Ireland

"As a parent, my only wish when my child started primary school was that they would be happy. Happiness as a child, one would imagine should be easily attainable but not so for the gifted learner. The frustration of being asked to do what seems to them like pointless exercises, the boredom in school, where everyone is treated as being the same out of fear of making one appear 'better', the differentiation of work that appears like a punishment (you are finished quickly so now do another twenty sums) – this approach can very quickly take their happiness away only to be replaced by frustration, anxiety and perfectionism, all topics which form essential reading in this welcome book. In short, the social and emotional development of our gifted learners is being seriously impacted by a system that is not meeting their needs. I applaud the author for bringing this important, timely and progressive publication to the public domain."

Claire Urquert, Ireland
Parent of a gifted learner

"In this book, Fidelma Healy Eames addresses the elusive nature of definitions of giftedness and presents potential support tools for parents and teachers, along with examining some of the major challenges concerning identification and the manifestation of gifted traits. As an extremely underrepresented category of special educational need in Ireland, gifted and twice exceptional students suffer in the absence of understanding, and so this book opens further channels to discourse that will support gifted individuals, parents, and teachers, seeking to gain a greater understanding of giftedness and twice exceptionality."

Dr Muireann O'Sullivan-Byrne, Ireland
Primary teacher and researcher

"This book is a great resource for parents and teachers of gifted learners. It helps identify the gifted child and provides strategies to help them be successful. Throughout, there are many anecdotal stories about gifted students that are enlightening. It is clear that the author has done significant research and spent a great deal of time interviewing gifted learners, their parents and teachers. The many viewpoints are fascinating and provide useful insights and information. I highly recommend it!"

Janet Davis, New York, USA
Elementary teacher and parent of gifted learner

Acknowledgments

My heart is full. I am honoured to express my gratitude to the many people who made this book possible. A two-and-a-half-year project, it started out with the series editor, Gavin Reid, asking me to write a book for the *How to Help* series about the gifted learner. Without your request Gavin this book would not exist.

That marked the beginning of my journey to source the fifty-four gifted learners, parents and nominated teachers that I interviewed for this book. And what a learning journey that has been! Huge thanks are due to those who helped me identify gifted learners – Colm O'Reilly (CTYI) and Marie Killilea being some of those who introduced me to talented learners and their families. This book is a credit to all of you – learners, parents and teachers. Your interest was enormous, your insights were invaluable. Respect… through you I learned what it means to be a gifted learner.

Not forgetting the many who supported me along the way. To Jimmy Deenihan for introducing me to Noelle Campbell Sharp and the Cill Rialaig project (Ballinskellig, Co. Kerry) for facilitating an inspirational writers' retreat for the month of July 2021. I will never forget it. And especially to my good friends Sandra Ryan, Rosabelle O'Donnell Burke and Aideen O'Mahoney who visited me there, encouraged me and kept my nose to the grindstone. The River Mill Writers' Retreat (Co. Down) provided another such useful sanctuary later in the year.

To Helen Hancock, Gina Mannion and Gavin for their early readings and responses to my calls.

To my family Michael, Ruth and Niall for understanding the importance of this book and the many drafts strewn on various tables! I sensed that patience was strained when hubby advised me to 'finish the book before you come home'. If only…

It would be remiss of me not to acknowledge Darren Reed and the editorial staff at Pavilion publishing for their generous and helpful critique. This book is stronger because of your guidance.

It is my fervent hope that this book will enhance the lives and experiences of our gifted and talented learners and become a useful resource for parents, caregivers and teachers alike.

Míle buíochas ó chroí,

Fidelma

How to Use This Book

Topics in this *How to Help* book are organised within five major sections, comprising parts 2 to 6:

- Learning characteristics
- Creativity
- Motivation and leadership
- Social and emotional development
- Inclusion and curriculum provision

Within these sections, each topic is discussed in a separate chapter (although it should be noted that in practice there will frequently be areas of overlap), with advice for parents, caregivers, teachers and schools. You can read through the sections in order or go straight to what concerns you most. The topics have been chosen to represent the key issues that research has indicated as being essential to an understanding of gifted learners, and how their needs can be accommodated and fulfilled.

 Whenever you see the *How to Help* icon, you can expect to find practical, ready to use suggestions and strategies for helping children and young people to grow in confidence and competence, to understand and accept themselves, to thrive and succeed.

We recommend that you read in full the Introduction (Part 1) and the Conclusion (Part 7). The former serves as an entry point into the main chapters, presenting the subject, models of giftedness and core principles along with a list of ten essential things to know. The latter summarises the most important points for readers to take away and offers final comments for parents, caregivers, teachers and schools.

To keep up to date with the *How to Help* series, bookmark:
www.pavpub.com/howtohelp

*"Hide not your talents.
They for use were made.
What's a sundial in the shade?"*

Benjamin Franklin

Part 1: Introduction

Chapter 1: What is giftedness?

> **Key Point**
>
> *Very little time, attention and understanding is given to giftedness by education systems, in favour of the mainstream and the struggling learner.*

My lifelong interest has been in what makes learning easier and enables individuals to 'own' the learning process for themselves. Like many of the people I interviewed – individuals of various backgrounds, ages and experience, whose views and recollections will punctuate, colour and bring to life most of the chapters of this book – part of me initially felt that this was one area that gifted learners didn't have to worry about. When I listened and reflected further, though, I realised that giftedness was one end of the learning spectrum that was quite neglected. Very little time, attention and consequently understanding is given to giftedness by teachers and education systems, in favour of the mainstream and the struggling learner, So, perhaps I can be forgiven for not immediately noticing their neglect.

Perhaps you are a teacher with a gifted child in your class, or a parent who suspects that your own child is gifted. Either way, what does that really mean? This book aims to do three things. Firstly, to enable parents and teachers to identify gifted learners in the home and school context. Secondly, to better understand them as learners and appreciate their learning differences, potential and challenges including the possibility of being 'twice-exceptional' (having giftedness and a learning difficulty). And thirdly, to be a 'how to help' resource for parents, teachers and caregivers to enable these learners to realise their vast potential.

A brief history of gifted learning

The events and thinking that have shaped our understanding of gifted learning over the last century are fascinating and inspirational. Today, gifted education has evolved into a complex educational discipline with well thought out pedagogy and research agendas. It has been argued that three major paradigm shifts in gifted education have been identified: demystification (i.e., giftedness as manifested wonders); identification (i.e., giftedness as measurable predictions); and transaction (i.e., creating and sustaining appropriate developmental niches for gifted individuals). A long time in the making, this is nevertheless a welcome and exciting realisation.

Only a century earlier, the early studies of giftedness evolved from research on mental inheritance, subnormal children, construction of instruments to measure both the sub and supernormal, and the realisation that graded schools could not adequately meet the needs of all children. This is still significant today. Pioneers such as the 'father of the gifted movement' Lewis Terman, who equated giftedness with high IQ, and Leta Hollingworth with her pioneering book *Gifted Children: Their Nature and Nurture*, spearheaded the movement and conducted some of the first widely published studies.

The field of gifted education continued to evolve through the twentieth century, mainly in America. The Soviet Union's launch of Sputnik in 1957 was significant. It spurred the US to act with a renewed awareness and interest in education for the gifted, particularly in the areas of maths and science. Legislative efforts by the federal government in the early 1970s brought the plight of gifted school children back into the spotlight.

By the 1980s, most investigators defined giftedness in terms of multiple qualities, not all of which were intellectual. IQ scores were becoming increasingly viewed as inadequate measures, and motivation, high self-concept and creativity were viewed as key qualities in the broadened conceptions of giftedness.[4] Howard Gardner's 1983 theory specifying eight different intelligences – linguistic, maths-logical, musical, spatial, bodily-kinaesthetic, interpersonal, intrapersonal and naturalist – attracted wide attention in the Western world, and served as an exciting example of the multi-faceted nature of intelligence and giftedness.[5]

Towards the close of the twentieth century, the *Jacob Javits Gifted and Talented Students Education Act (1988)* was passed to support the development of talent in American schools. Studies such as *A Nation at Risk and National Excellence: A Case for Developing America's Talent*, highlighted the missed opportunities to identify and serve gifted students, and the issuance of standards by the National Association for Gifted Children (NAGC) armed school districts across the country with a uniform set of criteria. Shortly after the turn of the millennium, *A Nation Deceived* reported on the advantages of acceleration for gifted children, illustrating America's inability to properly meet the needs of its most able students despite the overwhelming research supporting acceleration and enrichment.

---

4   Siegler, R.S. & Kotovsky, K. (1986) Two levels of giftedness: Shall ever the twain meet? In Sternberg, R.J. & Davidson, J.E. (Eds.) *Conceptions of giftedness*. Cambridge University Press.
5   Banks, F. & Mayes, A.S. (2001) *Early Professional Development for Teachers*. David Fulton.

The twenty-first century represents a new age where the possibilities and the future for gifted and talented learners are limitless and will hopefully become a priority for all countries at national and international levels. The most important turning point in gifted and talented education in the early twenty-first century has been an understanding of the multi-dimensionality of giftedness as many, varied and unique.[6] Quite simply, gifted learners are too important a resource to be treated as 'all the same'.

More detailed information on key dates and milestones in gifted education across a selection of countries can be found in Appendix 3.

Defining giftedness

A review of the literature reveals several definitions of giftedness and gifted learners that may help us with our understanding. None are universally agreed upon, but many of them share characteristics that are helpful. In this section I will share four separate definitions of giftedness, each of which has aspects that resonate for different reasons and each of which I drew upon to construct my own Gifted Learner Framework (GLF).

Definition 1

Some definitions of giftedness address the 'asynchronous development' found in gifted children. One comes from the Columbus Group:[7]

> *"Giftedness is asynchronous development in which advanced cognitive abilities and heightened intensity combine to create inner experiences and awareness that are qualitatively different from the norm. This asynchrony increases with higher intellectual capacity. The uniqueness of the gifted renders them particularly vulnerable and requires modifications in parenting, teaching and counselling in order for them to develop optimally."*

This is also the definition used by the Institute for Educational Advancement (IEA). I like it because it captures the uneven development of gifted learners, and the advanced pace of their learning and development compared with their peers. It also recognises the heightened intensity and vulnerability that are common features of many gifted learners, and the need for different approaches to parenting and teaching for their optimal development.

---

6   Vahidi, S. (2015). *Major Turning Points in Gifted Education in the 20th Century*. Renzulli Center for Creativity, Gifted Education, and Talent Development [online].

7   Columbus Group (1991) Unpublished transcript of the meeting of the Columbus Group, cited in Silverman, L.K. (1997). The Construct of Asynchronous Development. *Peabody Journal of Education*, 72(3&4), 36-58.

Definition 2

In the USA, the *Jacob Javits Gifted & Talented Students Education Act, NAGC (1988)* is the only federal program dedicated specifically to gifted and talented students.[8] It defines gifted students as:

> *"Students, children, or youth who give evidence of high achievement capability in areas such as intellectual, creative, artistic, or leadership capacity, or in specific academic fields, and who need services and activities not ordinarily provided by the school in order to fully develop those capabilities."*

This definition is important because it notes that giftedness can exist in specific fields and does not necessarily have to apply across the board. It is vital that we acknowledge 'stand-out giftedness' in particular fields, such as music, language, mathematics or leadership. That is not to say that these learners do not perform very well in other areas too, but they may not be 'cross-talented' (talented across all domains) – and they don't need to be in order to be considered gifted. This is an essential point for teachers and parents to be aware of.

Most US states also have their own definition of 'gifted' for programme and funding purposes. However, few districts differentiate between the different levels of giftedness.[9] For example, a child who scores in the 130-140 range on an IQ test is very different to a child who scores in the 150-180 range. More research is needed in this area.

Definition 3

In her book *Gifted Children: Myths and Realities*, Professor Ellen Winner defines giftedness with these three exceptional characteristics:[10]

- Gifted children are precocious – *"They begin to take the first steps in the mastery of some domain at an earlier-than-average age. They also make more rapid progress in this domain than do ordinary children, because learning in the domain comes easily to them."*
- They insist on marching to their own drum – *"Gifted children not only learn faster than average or even bright children but also learn in a quantitatively different way."*

---

8   National Association for Gifted Children (1988). *Frequently Asked Questions about Gifted Education* [online].
9   VanTassel-Baska, J. (2006) A Content Analysis of Evaluation Findings Across 20 Gifted Programs: A Clarion Call for Enhanced Gifted Program Development. *Gifted Child Quarterly*, 50(3), 199-215.
10 Winner, E. (1996) *Gifted Children: Myths and Realities*. Basic Books.

- They demonstrate a 'rage to master' – *"Gifted children are intrinsically motivated to make sense of the domain in which they show precocity."*

This is a very interesting definition in that it drills down into the unique and exceptional characteristics of gifted learners such as evidence of early learning and mastery and intrinsic motivation for learning's sake. These features are evident in some of the learners interviewed for this book.

Definition 4

The National Association for Gifted Children (NAGC) in the United States defines giftedness in the following way:[11]

"Gifted individuals are those who demonstrate outstanding levels of aptitude (defined as an exceptional ability to reason and learn) or competence (documented performance or achievement in top 10% or rarer) in one or more domains. Domains include any structured area of activity with its own symbol system (e.g., mathematics, music, language) and/or set of sensorimotor skills (e.g., painting, dance, sports)."

This is a definition of giftedness that is more commonly understood by teachers and educators who expect the performance of gifted learners to be in the top ten percent in one or more specific fields. The exceptional reasoning ability of gifted learners is remarkable. It is encouraging to note that giftedness is not limited exclusively to academic excellence, and that skills such as painting, dance and sport are also acknowledged – skills that add value and colour and connect uniquely with the human condition and the diversity of society today. In addition to being very efficient learners, many of the learners I interviewed have gifts in these areas.

---

11 Grier, J.E. (2020) *Effectively Implementing Gifted Education for Overlooked Students in PA: Examination and Recommendations for Modification of PA. Code 22 Ch. 16.* ERIC [online].

Chapter 2: Why do gifted learners matter?

In the same way that we aim to help all children grow through education, gifted learners have a right to be treated as individuals – to be identified, understood and enabled to reach their potential. Understanding their minds, their imagination, if that is possible, how they process, and the stresses and pressures they place on themselves to achieve is a feat in itself. As the Institute for Educational Advancement (IEA) states, what is important is that we identify these highly able young people and help them to reach their full intellectual, creative and personal potential.[12]

> ### Expert View
> "Students who are gifted are perhaps the most under-served population, and as a result at-risk population, in our schools today."
>
> Jennifer Katz

The teacher, author and advocate of inclusive education Jennifer Katz goes further in highlighting the neglect of gifted learners, its potential impacts and the urgent need for change.[13] She points out that students who are gifted are often dismissed as lucky, and denied specialised provision. The result, she argues, is a growing rate of mental health issues among this population including depression, substance abuse and adolescent suicide.

Why gifted learners merit study

Gifted learners are a unique group totalling no more than ten percent of the population, but with enormous potential if developed and nurtured – not just for themselves and for their families, but also for the contribution they can make to the wider world.[14] This makes them unique and 'special'. I use the word 'special' carefully, because it is largely used in relation to learners at the other end of the spectrum, namely those individuals who struggle to learn and are often categorised as having 'Special Educational Needs' (SEN).[15] In reality, both these groups are 'special' and the

---

12 Institute for Educational Advancement (2012). *5 Definitions of Giftedness*. [online]
13 Katz, J. (2013). *UDL & Gifted Education*. Threeblockmodel.com [online].
14 Bélanger, J. & Gagné, F. (2006). Estimating the Size of the Gifted/Talented Population from Multiple Identification Criteria. *Journal for the Education of the Gifted* 30 (2), 131-163.
15 Tony, C. & Norah, F. (2009) *Special Educational Needs, Inclusion and Diversity*. McGraw-Hill

mainstream classroom is more than challenged to meet the needs of each. Both groups require and deserve special attention and resourcing.

For children in the lower range with SEN, this is rightly being addressed to much greater effect today, after decades of neglect across education systems. However, as this book unfolds it will become obvious that the majority view among those interviewed is that special attention and resourcing is also essential for those in the upper range. Gifted children, no matter how we define or identify them, have different educational needs to their peers and their education must allow them to grow in tandem with their unique intellectual development.[12] At present, far too often this is sorely lacking.

This brings me to my second, and some might argue most important reason as to why gifted learners merit study – namely for the contribution they can make to the quality of life in their country, and to the wider world. They are essentially our 'seed potatoes'. When speaking with Colm O'Reilly, Director of the Centre for Talented Youth Ireland (CTYI), he said "Giftedness is frequently perceived as a first world problem", and indeed it may. Still, gifted learners have the potential to be multipliers and are always worth investing in. The payback at a global level is potentially huge.

In 2013, while a member of the Oireachtas (Irish Parliament), I was nominated to visit the headquarters of the Organisation for Economic Co-operation and Development (OECD) in Paris for a briefing on learning outcomes and how Ireland fared in comparison with other developed countries. I took away two very important messages:

- The higher a nation's learning outcomes, the more successful it will be in GDP terms, i.e., there is a direct relationship between educational success and national success.
- Ireland's top ten percent of learners needed to perform higher for Ireland to do better as a nation.

I was not surprised by the first point, but I was struck by the second. This has been reiterated in a recent TIMSS (Trends in International Mathematics and Science Study) report in relation to the under-performance of Ireland's top performers.[16] While Irish students are currently the top performers in mathematics in the European Union, when one drills into the data this is not the case for its top performers or gifted learners. In essence, the Irish education system is failing gifted learners.

As one wise teacher interviewed for this book advised, *"Gifted learners are too frequently left to their own devices; they need and deserve to be taught"*. The

---

16 Mullis, I.V.S., Martin, M.O., Foy, P., Kelly, D.L. & Fishbein, B. (2020). *TIMSS 2019 International Results in Mathematics and Science.* TIMSS & PIRLS International Study Center [online].

TIMSS study highlights that the world's top performers in both maths and science are largely Asian-based – coming from Singapore, Hong Kong, South Korea, Japan and Taiwan (in varying order). A study of the programmes that these countries offer is surely merited, but is beyond the scope of this book.

Thus, the evidence reveals that as a nation, Ireland is not maximising the potential of its gifted learners.[17] But this story is far from unique to Ireland.[18] When this happens, we all lose out. Gifted learners are our future researchers, our statisticians, our creators and our top scientists – they are crucial to research and innovation, to the knowledge economy and to the enhancement of society for the whole of the population.

> **Key Point**
>
> *Gifted learners are our future researchers, our statisticians, our creators and our top scientists – they are crucial to the enhancement of society.*

For too long, meeting the needs of gifted learners has simply been left to the creativity of the parent or the ingenuity of the teacher who is already stretched with large classes, presenting a myriad of needs. This is inadequate support. My research points to the urgent need for high-quality training for teachers at in-career and pre-service levels, including support programmes for parents, so that the gifted learner can be identified, recognised, understood and supported.

The Gifted Learner Framework (GLF)

While no two definitions of giftedness that we looked at in Chapter 1 are exactly the same, there are a number of recurring themes and guiding principles that can inform our thinking and understanding. Drawing upon this awareness and the various strands of giftedness, I constructed a Gifted Learner Framework (GLF) around the following six categories:

- Learning characteristics
- Creativity
- Maths and science
- Motivation
- Self-esteem (social and emotional development)
- Leadership

---

17 O'Reilly, C. (2005) Maximising potential – both academic and social–emotional. In: Smith, C. [Ed.] *Including the Gifted and Talented*. Routledge.
18 McGrath, P. (2018). Education in Northern Ireland: Does it meet the needs of gifted students? *Gifted Education International* [online].

The GLF lists a range of behaviours that have been identified in the literature as indicative of giftedness. Learners are not expected to demonstrate *all* these characteristics, however. This is a framework for considering the ways in which learners think and behave. Learners too can use the framework as a reference to think about their own stand-out features, what fulfils them as a learner and why, and what doesn't help them learn and why. This information will help teachers and educators to establish a more accurate picture of them, both as an individual and as a learner.

The Gifted Learner Framework (GLF)

Learning characteristics	Creativity	Maths and science
The learner shows: ■ Superior reasoning powers ■ Outstanding problem-solving ability ■ Ability to see subtle relationships ■ Persistent intellectual curiosity; questioning ■ Grasp of underlying principles; ability to make generalisations ■ Avid reading, absorbing books well beyond years ■ Ready understanding, quick learning and knowledge retention ■ Flexibility in thinking; considers problems from multiple angles	*The learner shows:* ■ Superior quality and quantity of written and/or spoken vocabulary and usage ■ Creative ability and expression in areas such as music, art, dance, drama, sport ■ Sensitivity and finesse in rhythm, movement, and body control ■ Originality in creative/intellectual work ■ Keen observation and responsiveness to new ideas ■ Alertness, with subtle sense of humour ■ Evidence of divergent thinking	*The learner shows:* ■ Insight into mathematical problems that require careful reasoning ■ Ability to grasp mathematical concepts readily ■ Curiosity about how things work, asks searching questions ■ Ability to grasp scientific concepts readily ■ Enjoyment when working with mathematical and/or scientific concepts
Motivation	Self-esteem (social and emotional development)	Leadership
The learner shows: ■ Awareness that school is linked to life purpose ■ Outstanding responsibility and independence in classroom work	*The learner shows:* ■ Perfectionism ■ Intensity ■ Over-excitability ■ Self-acceptance, ease and social poise	*The learner shows:* ■ Ability to carry responsibility well ■ Sociability and an outgoing attitude ■ Self-confidence with peers and adults

■ Ability to sustain concentration for long periods of time ■ Initiative in intellectual work ■ Boredom with schoolwork ■ Competitiveness	■ Tendency to be overly self-critical in evaluating/correcting own efforts ■ Ability to set realistically/ unrealistically high standards for self ■ Proneness to worry and anxiety ■ Social isolation/ loneliness ■ Difficulty 'fitting in' ■ Tendency to be teased and/or bullied	■ Ability to communicate with adults in a mature way ■ Interest in world problems and in solving them ■ Honesty and transparency

Figure 2.1: The Gifted Learner Framework (Healy Eames, 2020)

The GLF was a useful tool when conducting the case study interviews for this book – it provided a common basis for conversation about the person at the centre of the process, namely the gifted learner. A separate questionnaire was also attached for each party (learner, parent and teacher – see Appendices 6-8) to elicit key information aimed at better understanding and helping the gifted learner.

The interview process was thorough; all interviews were conducted online, with each lasting approximately one-and-a-quarter hours and the longest stretching to almost two hours. At times the interviews became quite therapeutic for both the learners and their parents, with some learners saying that *"every learner should have this experience."* It was encouraging to find that, through this framework, the gifted learners felt heard and understood. It was also fulfilling to hear some parents say about the GLF: *"I felt you were describing my child."*

Chapter 3: Models of giftedness

When I interviewed the mother of twelve-year-old **Dylan**, she made an impactful pitch on the need for gifted learners to be 'seen'. When I probed this further, she explained: *"To have your needs met, you need to be identified as having them in the first place."* She continued: *"Being seen is not just passive. It is being understood and not just acknowledged. When you're understood, your needs are too."* She summed up the first two aims of this book perfectly, and of course this awareness leads us to reflect on the implications for teaching, learning and parenting too.

> ### Expert View
> *"Being seen is not just passive. It is being understood and not just acknowledged. When you're understood, your needs are too."*
>
> Mother of Dylan, age 12

We have definitions of giftedness and test scores that can indicate giftedness. The case studies in this book will highlight that giftedness can be recognised by teachers and parents and through the feedback of significant others. But is there an empirical basis available to help identify gifted learners? The answer is yes – there are models available to help us understand giftedness and more easily identify the gifted learner. In this chapter we examine five well-known models of giftedness, and consider how they relate to the Gifted Learner Framework (GLF) introduced in Chapter 2.

The three-ring model of giftedness

Created by the American educational psychologist Joe Renzulli, the three-ring model of giftedness was used to identify and inform a programme for one of our interviewed gifted learners, **Jess**, in her school in New York state. The model documents three interconnected factors, namely: i. above average ability; ii. creativity; and iii. task commitment.[19] These factors share much common ground with the GLF.

---

19 Renzulli, J. S. (2016) The three-ring conception of giftedness: A developmental model for promoting creative productivity. In: *Reflections on gifted education: Critical works by Joseph S. Renzulli and colleagues* (pp.55-90). Prufrock Press.

Figure 3.1: The three-ring model of giftedness

Within 'Above Average Ability', Renzulli distinguishes between general abilities (e.g., processing information, integrating experiences, abstract thinking) and specific abilities (e.g., the capacity to perform in an activity). This compares well with the 'Learning Characteristics' section of the GLF for general abilities, whereas the 'specific ability' performance is indicated in the GLF's 'Creativity' and 'Maths and Science' sections.

Within 'Creativity', Renzulli lists fluency, flexibility, originality of thought, openness to experience, sensitivity to stimulations, and willingness to take risks. Similarities can be found here to the 'Creativity' section of the GLF.

Within 'Task Commitment', Renzulli understands motivation turned into action (like perseverance, endurance, hard work, but also self-confidence, perceptiveness and a special fascination with a specific subject). This concept is significant, and it is captured in the application sections of the GLF under 'Motivation', 'Self-Esteem' and 'Leadership'. Renzulli argues that without task commitment, high achievement is simply not possible.

My interviews revealed that task commitment is an innate feature of many gifted learners as they grow, develop and move along their educational journey. They may be able to perform well naturally early and at primary level, but beyond this they really appear to apply pressure on themselves to maintain a high-level of performance, particularly as the pool of learners widens. **Jude**'s father was adamant that commitment and application were the key factors for his son achieving high performance and developing natural ability. This is interesting as it debunks the myth that gifted learners are 'born'.

According to Renzulli's model, only if characteristics from all three rings work together can high achievement or gifted behaviour result. More recently, Renzulli has shifted emphasis towards background factors in his models – environmental factors and individual differences that influence gifted behaviour. This is a welcome development. The case studies bear out the wider impact of the home environment, parental awareness and the individual's personality in their development as a gifted learner.

The Munich model

The Munich Model of Giftedness (MMG) uses a multifactorial approach to explain giftedness and its development. It draws its theoretical perspective from one of the largest surveys of gifted adolescents in Europe, and has been internationally validated in several studies.[20] It is based on four interdependent dimensions: i. talent factors (relatively independent); ii. resulting performance areas; iii. personality factors; and iv. environmental factors. The latter two dimensions moderate the transition from talent (gifts) to performance.[21]

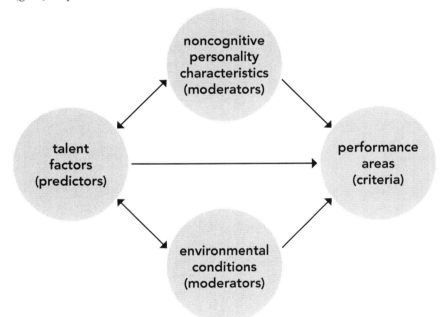

Figure 3.2: The Munich model of giftedness

---

20 Heller, K.A., Perleth, C. & Lim, T.K. (2005) The Munich Model of Giftedness Designed to Identify and Promote Gifted Students. *In Conceptions of Giftedness*, 2nd ed (pp. 147-170). Cambridge University Press.

21 Giger, M. (2006) *The Munich Model of Giftedness* [online].

The model consists of seven relatively independent ability factor groups or gifted predictors (intellectual abilities; creative abilities; social competence; practical intelligence; artistic abilities; musicality; psychomotor skills) and eight performance domains where the giftedness might be seen (maths; natural sciences; technology; computer science; arts; languages; sports; social relationships). There are also important non-cognitive personality characteristics (e.g. coping with stress; achievement motivation; learning and working strategies; control expectations; hopes for success versus fear of failure; thirst for knowledge; self-concept) and environmental conditions (family climate; number of siblings and sibling position; parental education level; home environmental stimulation; home demands regarding performance; familiar learning environment; classroom climate; quality of instruction; differentiated learning and instruction; educational style; social reactions to success and failure; critical life events) that are moderated by the talent factors, and that in themselves moderate talent and performance.

This interplay of factors in the MMG highlights the complexity of giftedness in and of itself. It shows that giftedness is the product of many factors coming together (talent factors resulting in performance areas, moderated by personality traits and environmental conditions) and the complexity of these conditions can result in a miracle of sorts. Notably, the MMG can perhaps explain why some children identified as having extraordinary ability don't realise their potential in terms of performance – it may be the impact of the moderating personality and environmental factors. The interview schedules attaching to the GLF provided a useful starting point for discussing environmental conditions at home and in school with learner, parent and teacher.

The differentiated model

The Differentiated Model of Giftedness and Talent (DMGT) developed by the French-Canadian professor Françoys Gagné proposes a clear distinction between the two most basic concepts of giftedness and talent in the field of gifted education, and is the most widely accepted definition in Australia today.[22] Under the DMGT, giftedness is defined as:

> "*The possession and use of untrained and spontaneously expressed superior natural abilities (called aptitudes or gifts), in at least one ability domain, to a degree that places an individual at least among the top ten percent of his or her age peers.*"

---

22 Gagne, F. (2000) *A Differentiated Model of Giftedness and Talent.* Year 2000 Update. ERIC [online].

The DMGT proposes four aptitude domains for giftedness: i. intellectual; ii. creative; iii. socio-affective; and iv. sensorimotor. These natural abilities, the development and level of expression of which is partly controlled by the individual's genetic endowment, can be observed in many tasks that children are confronted with over the course of their schooling.

The DMGT follows what might be considered a 'traditional' understanding of giftedness in that it points to abilities with which individuals are naturally endowed genetically, leading the gifted learner to perform among the top ten percent in at least one field. Similarly, when identifying gifted learners for this book, I required that they have a specific ability or gift manifested as stand-out performance in at least one area. The learner did not need to be 'cross-talented' or gifted in all areas, although some of the learners interviewed did appear to meet this criterion (e.g. **Rhys**, **Ava**).

In the course of my study, I encountered an eleven-year-old boy who had an extraordinary command of spoken and written language and a remarkable ability to integrate prior reading into his writing. Yet his teacher did not view him as gifted because he lacked equal prowess in maths. To not consider a child with a stand-out ability in one area as gifted is to miss identifying him and risk not enabling his potential. In life and work we tend to specialise mainly in one area, and we don't require gifts across all domains. Moreover, recognition of a specific ability may be the catalyst that enables a gifted learner to develop abilities in other areas. I was particularly cognisant of this when concluding that giftedness could be in one specific domain only.

The WICS model

WICS is an acronym for Wisdom-Intelligence-Creativity-Synthesized.[23] According to the model's developer Robert Sternberg, when we identify individuals as gifted, we often neglect what is perhaps the most important dimension of all: giftedness for leadership. He argues that there is a big difference between knowing a lot about a field and taking a leadership role, and ultimately gifted individuals should not just be 'good' – they should be potential leaders in one or more domains. Sternberg contends that effective leaders demonstrate a synthesis of three elements: creativity, intelligence and wisdom. Creativity is used to generate ideas; intelligence is used to analyse and implement them and persuade others of their worth; and wisdom is used to balance the effects on all possible stakeholders.

This model appealed to me for two main reasons. Firstly, because I interviewed five gifted adult learners (**Melissa**, **Greg**, **Miguel**, **Jess** and

---

23 Sternberg, R. J. (2005) WICS: A model of giftedness in leadership. *Roeper Review* 28(1) 37-44.

Maria) whose gifts, in part at least, have translated into leadership roles in their adult lives. And secondly, because I believe teachers and parents should be more aware of the potential for leadership in gifted learners, particularly in their gifted area, and the special attention that this merits. Realisation of leadership potential does not mean that a learner will not experience challenges; rather, it highlights the extraordinary contribution that their gifts can make to life and society. This is also why leadership is a key section in the GLF.

The AMR Method

The Roeper School for the Gifted in Michigan was one of the first schools for gifted children in the US, founded more than seventy-five years ago. The Annemarie Roeper (AMR) Method of Qualitative Assessment, created by its founder, is a comprehensive model that draws on qualitative assessments to arrive at a cohesive picture of a gifted child.[24] Roeper says:

> *"The human psyche is one of enormous complexity, not fully measurable by standardized psychometric examinations. The only instrument complex enough to understand a human being is another human being. AMR Method practitioners use themselves as the instrument through which to understand the child or adult."*

Using the AMR Method, practitioner judgements are informed by observing the child's behaviour before and during the assessment. Children who say "approximately" or "precisely" show advanced language development, regardless of their actual scores. The IQ scores of parents or siblings, early achievement of developmental milestones, profound curiosity, deep moral concern, remarkable associations or generalisations, perfectionism, keen attention to detail, vivid imagination, unusual empathy, superb memory, advanced vocabulary, early reading or fascination with Lego, school achievement, reading interests and parental anecdotes of precocious reasoning are all taken seriously in determining the abilities of a child.

Experienced practitioners use this information to create a composite picture of the level of the child's abilities. IQ test results are then nested into this schema to add further information. The AMR Method is not reliant on traditional testing alone and offers a unique approach to evaluation for giftedness. Its level of qualitative detail is evident within and across the six sections of the GLF and was used to frame the interviews for this book.

---

24   Roeper, A. (2016) The Annemarie Roeper Method of Qualitative Assessment: My Journey. Roeper Review 38(4).

Summary

All five models outlined here offer helpful insights for identifying and understanding the gifted learner. Heller's Munich model provides a useful framework for the breadth of understanding of giftedness that needs to be considered, and Roeper's AMR Method elucidates the depth of observable detail that can identify a learner as 'different'. Renzulli's three-ring model results from a dynamic interaction of above-average general ability, high levels of creativity and task commitment, and like Gagné's differentiated model it recognises that a range of factors must be in place for students with natural abilities to develop their gifts into high levels of performance. Finally, Sternberg's WICS model stresses how giftedness can manifest over time not just in high performance, but also in leadership.

Taken together, the five models indicate broad agreement that a decisive factor in the determination of effective gifted learning is the fit between individual factors on the one hand, and environmental influences on the other. These factors have implications for the development of gifted education programmes, which will be addressed as this book unfolds.

Chapter 4: Testing and assessment

This chapter explores the use of testing and assessment to identify gifted and talented learners. The subject of giftedness, and the reliance on tests alone for the identification of gifted learners, has always been controversial. Some thinkers including Professor James Borland have pointed to an over-reliance on IQ and traditional methods of identification, and the need to consider alternative ways of thinking about gifted education.[25]

> ## Expert View
>
> *"There is a canon of research on high performance, built over the last century, that suggests it goes way beyond tested intelligence."*[27]
>
> Wendy Berliner

While many schools do use multiple measures and assess a wide variety of talents, including verbal, mathematical, spatial-visual, musical, and interpersonal, there can still be an over-reliance on ability tests, with the prevailing measure of giftedness considered to be an IQ of 130 or more.

Why test?

Testing is orderly in many respects. It offers an objective, systematic way to identify gifted children. Ability and achievement tests provide scores to pinpoint a student's performance in relation to their peers. Teachers and schools often use these tests to benchmark entry into specific programmes, and to identify specific learning difficulties such as dyslexia. However, formal assessments are only one tool in determining giftedness; educators should create a challenging environment and collect multiple types of information so that all students are able to demonstrate their gifts and talents.[27,28] This is particularly needed to identify students who may be excluded – for example English language learners, disabled learners or students from minority or low-income backgrounds.

Another good reason for testing is that there is a difference between giftedness and high-achievement potential. As the author Christopher Taibbi has stated, *"a bright child knows the answer, the gifted learner asks*

---

25 Borland, J.H. [ed] (2003) *Rethinking Gifted Education*; Teacher's College Press
26 Berliner, W. (2017) Why there's no such thing as a gifted child. *The Guardian* [online].
27 National Association for Gifted Children (2022) *Tests & Assessments* [online].
28 National Association for Gifted Children (2022) *Standard 2: Assessments* [online].

the questions".[29] A bright child generally needs six to eight repetitions to learn something; a gifted child needs one or two. They may both achieve good grades but their mental process has been different.[30] This became obvious when I interviewed **Jess**'s teacher about her exceptional maths ability. She said, *"The answer just appears for the gifted child, she wouldn't necessarily be able to explain how that happened"*. Later, becoming a tutor of other students at secondary level helped Jess to develop this skill.

It is also important to distinguish between testing and assessment. Tests are administered in a standardised, scripted way to ensure scientific neutrality in scoring, whereas assessments may include a standardised or IQ test but also go beyond that. For example, children can be interviewed and children's play is sometimes used to make judgements about development. In the case of assessment, the assessor's point of view influences their decision about the learner. While tests can help to determine a learner's aptitudes so we can better respond to their individual learning needs, in general they are best used in conjunction with more subjective assessment tools.

Types of tests

Testing should be focused and aligned with the specific characteristics of gifted students – for example intellectual, creative, leadership, and specific academic fields such as maths, science and language. By extension, this would require more than one test to identify a gifted learner. Tests generally fall into two categories – ability tests and achievement tests.

Ability tests

IQ (Intelligence Quotient) test scores or cognitive ability test scores are frequently used to identify gifted students. These focus on everything from verbal reasoning to memory and processing speed. They provide useful information in intellectual domains, but they are not able to identify an individual with, for example, creative or leadership talent.

IQ test results are banded to determine giftedness in some children:

- ✔ Mildly gifted: 115-129
- ✔ Moderately gifted: 130-144
- ✔ Highly gifted 145-159

---

29 Taibbi, C. (2012) 'Bright Child' vs 'Gifted Learner': What's the Difference? *Psychology Today* [online].
30 Kingore, B. (2004) *High Achiever, Gifted Learner, Creative Learner* [online].

- ✔ Exceptionally gifted: 160-179
- ✔ Profoundly gifted: 180+

Most learners are in the 'normal' range of 85-115, with 100 as the absolute norm. The farther from 100 a child is, the greater the need for educational accommodations, regardless of whether the score is lower or higher. This is an important pointer when differentiating for educational provision.

Typical individual tests include the Stanford-Binet (SB5, Form L-M), the Weschler Intelligence Scale for Children (WISC-V) and the Woodcock-Johnson Tests of Cognitive Ability (WJ IV COG). However, it is rare for a school to administer any individual test of ability or intelligence unless the parent pays for the test privately or the child is referred to a psychologist. In the Irish context, the latter normally only takes place where the school has concerns about progress, i.e. lack of improvement.

Primary and secondary level students are typically tested using group testing methods at grade/class level or through their school's gifted and talented screening programme, where one exists.

Group tests include:

- CogAT (Cognitive Abilities Test) – a group administered test made up of verbal, quantitative and nonverbal batteries. Each contains three types of questions that cover unique cognitive abilities.
- Matrix Analogies Test – a screening test of nonverbal reasoning originally validated with US students. Items have a missing element, and the student selects the best option to completing the stimulus.
- Otis-Lennon School Ability Test (OLSAT) – assesses for higher order reasoning skills that involve analysis, synthesis and evaluation. It is a test of abstract thinking and reasoning ability of children.
- Ravens Progressive Matrices (RPM) – progressive matrices are used to assess cognitive ability in children and adults from a nonverbal perspective using geometric patterns with logical sequences.
- CAT4 test (GL assessment) – the UK and Ireland's most widely used test of reasoning abilities for children, measuring verbal, nonverbal, quantitative and spatial reasoning.

For culturally and linguistically diverse students or those from low-income backgrounds, the NAGC recommends the Naglieri Nonverbal Ability Test (NNAT3) and the Test of Nonverbal Intelligence (TONI-4) to mitigate the language barriers that may disadvantage these students.

Achievement tests

Achievement tests determine what a student has already learned and whether they are more advanced than their peers. For example, teachers would regularly glean information from standardised tests to see how their pupils perform compared to their peers in the norm group. The selected tests should not have a ceiling so that students can show all of what they know. This makes sense in that teachers and management can then determine the extent to which a pupil is ahead of their peer group and needs further provision.

Standardised tests that give wide-range results include the SAT (originally the Scholastic Aptitude Test, now simply the SAT, not to be confused with the National Curriculum SATs used in England), the Iowa Test of Basic Skills (ITBS) and the Oxford University Maths Admission Test (MAT). Examples of tests specifically designed for gifted students include the Test of Mathematical Abilities for Gifted Students (TOMAGS-2) and the Screening Assessment for Gifted Elementary Students (SAGES02)

When to test

There are differing views on whether to test young children, but generally it is held that IQ tests for children under six years of age are not suitable in that it is difficult to make accurate determinations. Instead, it is wiser to use alternative measures of giftedness such as observations, portfolios, teacher-parent surveys and gifted characteristic checklists.[27] A checklist to collect information for informal assessment might look like this:

- ✔ Early use of advanced vocabulary
- ✔ Keen observation and curiosity
- ✔ Retention from varied sources of information
- ✔ Periods of intense concentration
- ✔ Ability to understand complex concepts
- ✔ Ability to perceive relationships and think abstractly
- ✔ A broad and changing spectrum of interests
- ✔ Strong critical thinking skills and self-criticism

Interpreting test scores

Tests should always be administered and interpreted by trained professionals. The test selected should relate to a specific area of giftedness. Tests provide a variety of scores – raw scores, percentile ranks, standard scores and grade-equivalent scores. Assessments should be current with recent norms and non-biased. It is vital to do a test review in advance of administering the test, and especially to review sub-scores. Sometimes, twice-exceptional students can be overlooked if only using a general score.

'Twice-exceptional' (2e) is a term used to describe learners who are gifted and also have a specific learning difficulty. Approximately one in six gifted learners falls into this category.[17] This finding points to the need for careful review and interpretation of test scores and sub-scores, so that exceptional abilities can be separated out from learning difficulties. Furthermore, it underlines how important it is that teachers have specific training and upskilling in this area. Teachers and other professionals can only look past a learning difficulty and recognise a child's potential if they are aware of it.

Results: what next?

Once the results of a test or assessment are in, the key question is what next? Ideally parents, teachers and management should use test data as one measure to inform and develop an appropriate educational strategy and programme of work for gifted students. But even when schools have access to results that raise awareness about students' unique abilities, it is still no guarantee that a programme will be implemented to cater for their needs – unless it is a mandated Department of Education requirement that is matched with appropriate teacher education upskilling.

The reality, based on the accounts of those interviewed for this book, is less than encouraging. Over and again, teachers revealed to me how it was left to their own intuitiveness and conscientiousness to find suitable resources and programmes to meet gifted students' needs and foster engagement. With the myriad of needs presenting in typical classes of around thirty students, this only happened in some cases. One mother spoke about regularly photocopying extra work for her child's teacher to keep her son occupied in class. Unsurprisingly, this wasn't always met with enthusiasm.

Clearly, provision at this ad hoc level is inadequate and demoralising for all parties involved. Governments worldwide need to be more proactive with training and programme development for gifted and talented learners in the best interests of children, teachers and parents. This is a key recommendation for policymakers and legislators arising from this book.

Ten key things to know about giftedness and gifted learners

1. Giftedness is multi-dimensional and exists in up to ten percent of the population.

2. Gifted learners demonstrate advanced learning in at least one field. These abilities are generally observable in the course of their schooling.

3. Gifted learners see the world differently; they pose different questions and have inner experiences that are qualitatively different from their peers.

4. Gifted learners require 'idea-mates' rather than 'age-mates' – intellectual peers who can grasp abstract ideas and get their jokes.

5. Gifted learners can sometimes under-achieve or become bored at school due to not being understood, or a lack of curriculum challenge.

6. Gifted learners can be prone to anxiety and self-imposed pressures, and function better when they are understood and can learn at a pace that is in keeping with their accelerated readiness to learn.

7. Leadership is a less recognised dimension of giftedness. This may be particularly apparent in the learner's gifted area and should be encouraged.

8. IQ has been the prevailing measure of giftedness but, ideally, ability tests should be used in conjunction with more subjective assessment tools.

9. Approximately one in six gifted learners also has a specific learning difficulty. These learners are termed 'twice-exceptional' (2e) and require informed responses.

10. Gifted and talented learners can make a positive difference to society. Governments worldwide need to proactively invest in them.

Part 2: Learning characteristics

Chapter 5: Curiosity

If giftedness is considered as a developmental process, then we might think of nurturing curiosity as its starting point. Giftedness is not entirely a chance event – it will blossom in those circumstances when children's cognitive ability, motivation and enriched environments coexist and meld together to foster its growth.[31] Curiosity has been defined as the recognition, pursuit and intense desire to explore novel, challenging and uncertain events.[32] Intellectually gifted students tend to show greater curiosity from infancy through to adolescence, and curiosity is also a fundamental predictor of the aspiration to become a scientist.[33]

> ### Expert View
>
> *"The important thing is to not stop questioning. Curiosity has its own reason for existing."*
>
> Albert Einstein

Persistent curiosity is a naturally occurring and invigorating feature of the gifted learners interviewed for this book. In every case, either the learner, their parent or teacher described them as curious and asking questions – some, admittedly, to a greater degree than others. Those especially interested in science had a curiosity about how things worked and were often referred to as 'asking searching questions'. This trait was omnipresent and impossible to ignore.

Scott Barry Kaufman stresses the benefits of curiosity in contributing not only to high achievement, but also to a fulfilling existence.[34] Curiosity has been linked to happiness, creativity, satisfying intimate relationships, increased personal growth after trauma and enhanced meaning in life. Yet, he points out, although research shows that curiosity is one of the strongest markers of academic success, it is underemphasised in the classroom.

Professor Susan Engel agrees. In her book *The Hungry Mind*, she argues that amidst the standardised testing mania, schools are missing what really matters about learning: the desire to learn in the first place.[35] She notes that

---

31 Gottfried, A.W., Gottfried, A.E., Bathurst, K. & Guerin, D.W. (1994) *Gifted IQ: Early Developmental Aspects – The Fullerton Longitudinal Study.* Springer.
32 Kashdan, T. & Silvia, P. (2009) Curiosity and Interest: The Benefits of Thriving on Novelty and Challenge. In *Oxford Handbook of Positive Psychology*, Oxford University Press.
33 Das, P. (2019) *Curiosity and passion are the keys to become a scientist... we need to create an environment that nurtures research.* Times of India Blog [online].
34 Kaufman, S.B. (2017) *Schools Are Missing What Matters About Learning.* The Atlantic [online].
35 Engel, S. (2015) *The Hungry Mind: The Origins of Curiosity in Childhood.* Harvard University Press.

teachers rarely encourage curiosity in the classroom – even though we are all born with abundant curiosity, and this innate drive to explore could be built upon in every student. Having a 'hungry mind' has been shown to be a core determinant of academic achievement, rivalling the predictive power of IQ. So it seems like our education systems may be missing out on one of the most innate gifts children are born with – curiosity and the desire to learn.

Curiosity as a driver of other traits

Curiosity manifests itself differently in individual learners. It is important to observe these patterns in the developing child, and to note the personality traits that develop as a result. **Ruby** is a case in point – an all-round gifted learner with particularly strong musical talent. Now twenty-four and a psychology graduate, she had a curious mind from an early age. In her mother's eyes she had a *"persistent, intellectual curiosity."*

Ruby developed leadership skills early. A twin, she was according to her mother, *"all adventure and discovery, and the leader of the two."* The outdoors provided her with endless hours of exploration, bringing in bugs from the garden for examination, the *"initiator of the games, always with her brother in tow"*. Interestingly, on speaking with Ruby, she classified leadership as her top strength after creative ability. This was recognised at school, where she was elected head girl and 'Student of the Year' in her final year. There she learned that she could *"mediate, multi-task easily and organise everything"*. When her teachers put her in an adult tutor role, she experienced more ownership and *"felt the purpose of learning in a different way than just sitting there learning for myself"*.

Ruby was a perfectionist who pursued things to the nth degree. Her mother noticed the link between curiosity and perfectionism. Musically gifted, at around the age of seven she found a website that taught her to yodel. She spent five hours practising until she perfected it. Today she still integrates yodelling and/or mimicking instruments into her musical performances.

Likewise, there is an obvious link between curiosity and problem-solving. When her mother lost a finger in an accident, while everyone else was panicking around her, Ruby, then only six, was questioning if it could be fixed. She was able to block out the drama and focus on finding a solution.

A gifted learner's natural curiosity and desire for challenge can lead to them discovering their niche. This is what happened to **Rhys**, sixteen, when he began to study Technical Graphics (TG). A gifted musician too, he initially chose to study music at school but found that he was not challenged by it. When he changed to TG, his innate curiosity about how things worked led him to innovate. Technology for him became a mix of learning to work with wood, metal, circuitry and electricity.

He realised he had an *"ability to grasp scientific concepts readily"* and loved physics because it was *"related to technology and electricity"*. This newly discovered talent is piquing his interest in *"creating different devices and high-end engineering"*. The study of aeronautical engineering as a course and potential career is currently holding a strong attraction for him. When I asked him how his mind works, he responded, *"I would visualise it and put it into real-life examples to make sense of it"*. Observing his growth as a learner, Rhys's mother said, *"I feel his giftedness is more pronounced now since he has become more independent and self-reliant as a learner"*.

Nurturing lifelong curiosity

Greg is forty-two and a psychologist, as well as a well-known motivational speaker and author. Listening to him, his curiosity about life and its meaning has become the bedrock of his career. *"My work today is still asking questions"*, he says. When I asked him what his talent was, he responded, *"The holistic development of the individual"*.

As a child his questions were always 'why' and 'how': *"Why are we born? Why do we die?"* He recalls getting lost in a supermarket and his mother finding him with a lonely figure. *"Why are you sad?"* he had asked the man. Little about his early schooling sparked interest in him; *"the conversations when school wasn't going well were what kept me at school"*. Poetry was the exception. Patrick Kavanagh's poetry was about his life, he says, *"We only see the world as we are. When I got to know the author and his life, I loved the open-ended question, 'what do you think he meant and why?'"*.

Greg's innate curiosity about the human condition has sparked a lifelong journey not just for himself but for others too, given his following. He says of studying for a Masters' degree in Counselling Psychology that he *"struggled with having to replicate the work of others; I wanted to define me and what I believed."*

Teachers really matter, he says. He references one teacher as among *"the most influential people in my life"* because *"she was the first person that was willing to understand me and work with me. She respected me and I respected her."* The connection was mutual. She described him as having *"the essence of realness at his core"*. The encounter came about as a result of his transferring to a different school. There he was struck by the *"mutual respect"* that was the hallmark of his new school. This, he said, developed trust between the students and teachers and, in his case, it led to him performing well. His teacher agrees: *"Everything flows from the understanding by the teacher"*, she said. It was to be a lucky coincidence.

Greg's mother described him as a very active child growing up, not at all interested in schoolwork. Within months of his final exams, a key moment changed him. Approaching him, his mother said, *"Gregory, your work is in your mind, so you'd better knuckle down and do well in your final exams. If you have to graft and do manual work, you'll starve."* This warning, she says, changed everything. After that, with the help of his teachers and family, Greg applied himself to his studies and achieved the results he needed to study Psychology and English in college.

Just as with Greg's teacher, whose respect for the learner and their mind was enormous, **Rhys**'s teacher approached her own teaching and learning with curiosity too. She adopted a 'no limits' approach that generated immense student engagement. She notes, *"the fact that Rhys realised he had total ownership of his own learning, that there were no limits, fulfilled him most of all."* This teacher was a gift, selected by Rhys as the stand-out teacher of his education to date. She posed constant challenges to his knowledge, for example saying, *"You don't believe everything you read, do you?"* It meant Rhys never assumed he knew anything and was always open to learning.

Her confidence and experience are evident: *"Show the children that you are wide open to getting things wrong"*, she advises. Teachers can regularly feel threatened, she warns, but if you adopt the approach of *"I don't have a clue how to get the answer, you give the learning over to the student"*. This approach works particularly well for gifted learners because their curiosity allows them to understand that knowledge is not fixed – that they can be the author, the creator, the diviner of the new knowledge themselves.

In one instance she invented a scenario made up of fact and fiction for the class. She gave students two weeks to research the scenario and discern what was truth and what was not. The scenario engaged the children and their families. Her objective was to teach her pupils to be critical thinkers, to read between the lines. When she revealed the full truth, some children were outraged and accused her of lying, whereas Rhys listened *"most respectfully"* and *"used logic"* to decipher the facts from the story.

A fan of mixed ability grouping and differentiating her teaching to suit the learner's needs, she says, *"I believe in fostering a 'forever learning' attitude, where none of us has a monopoly on knowledge and we learn together. I never use a schoolbook; I use whiteboards, real engagement and fun"*. While she draws on resources and equipment used in other education systems, she mostly believes that the best way for a teacher to extend the gifted learner is through learning approaches, ideas and a curious attitude.

How to help – curiosity

Strategies for parents and caregivers:

☞ Be open to learning, reading and finding out ways to support your gifted child. All children are different, so notice and follow their interests and let them guide you. Nurture their potential.

☞ Develop curiosity by exposing them to new experiences that make them curious (e.g. trips to the aquarium or museum). Don't worry if you can't answer all their questions; better still, look them up together.

☞ Observe your child's interests and facilitate them where possible, ideally before they become closed or hooked on gaming. Take note of requests for outdoor pursuits; they frequently know what suits them.

☞ Use the outdoors, nature, animals, pets, music, language, laughter and fun to engage them. Encourage a growth mindset so they come to understand that knowledge and learning isn't 'fixed'.

☞ Play with your child. Have fun exploring new frontiers together, and help them bridge the gap between dreaming and doing.

Strategies for teachers and schools:

☞ Approach teaching and learning with curiosity. Be curious about the children you teach, their interests and abilities. The gifted learner will love you for it. Notice their developing gifts and nurture their potential.

☞ Devise stimulating activities that offer novelty, complexity and surprise. Take things apart to see how they work. Create areas in the classroom where children can engage with different materials and resources.

☞ Encourage students to ask questions and challenge assumptions. Show them that this is the basis of the scientific mind. Give them problems to solve and stimulate divergent thinking with open-ended questions.

Ask the gifted learner how their mind works. This is revealing and will give you insights as to how they learn best and help them to become metacognitive observers of their own thinking and learning processes.

 Show respect for the learner and their mind – everything else will flow from that. A relationship of trust creates the path forward.

Chapter 6: Problem-solving

Gifted learners are curious beings who pose unforeseen questions with the ability to be selectively mentally engaged.[30] They relish a challenge and possess outstanding problem-solving ability, an aptitude particularly visible in maths and science. Research by Professor Lee Swanson revealed that gifted children used 'fewer moves' to solve a problem and exhibited high metacognitive knowledge on person and strategy variables compared with children of lower IQ, suggesting that the processing advantages may be related to a 'superior central processing system'.[36]

> ### Expert View
> *"Too often we give our children answers to remember rather than problems to solve."*
>
> Roger Lewin

Outstanding problem-solving ability was a stand-out feature across the gifted learners interviewed for this book. This chapter will consider gifted learners with remarkable problem-solving ability from primary school through to adulthood. Interestingly, while all the learners we look at 'loved' maths and science to varying extents, how they approached and used problem-solving can reveal itself differently.

Challenge seekers

Gifted learners crave a challenge. Not just for the sake of it – it is an innate need, a thirst that must be satisfied. When I asked **Jess**, aged twenty-nine, what fulfilled her as a learner she recalled a teacher who *"adapted the work to make things challenging for me."* Her gifted learner programme teacher remarked on the tenacity of gifted learners: *"they stick with the problem, even if they don't get it right first time."*

Luka, a twenty-four-year-old graduate of Music and French, recalls the satisfaction he got when he was given a challenge at the age of eleven to design a trip to Warsaw for his whole class *"from start to finish."* For him it wasn't just content he learned; he developed new skills that he used later to complete tasks. Luka was ready early for complex, individual projects. His mother recalls: *"he always had his own way of learning – he'd ask and we'd follow; he never wanted a challenge to get the better of him; I could visibly see him thinking."* **Olga**'s teacher highlighted that gifted learners' thirst for problem-solving makes for *"different gravy"*

---

36 Swanson, H. L. (1992). The relationship between metacognition and problem solving in gifted children. *Roeper Review*, 15(1), 43–48.

entirely. She advises teachers to be careful to *"keep the balance of challenge and being a child."*

Pushing forward

Lucy, aged eleven, a highly intense child, was instructive regarding problem-solving: *"I'm not looking for extra work, I just want harder work – I want a challenge. In third and fourth grade the teacher gave me the easy work first, then the problem-solving. I would prefer to go straight to the hard work, rather than do a ton of work, most of which I find easy."* Lucy ranked in the ninety-ninth percentile. Her teacher noted that she got the last question right in the 'Micra-T' test whereas *"most kids don't."*

Describing her interests, Lucy said: *"I'm good at maths and art, I love science experiments and maths games but not when I'm just writing out sums! Maths games like 'mathletics' on the iPad are so satisfying. It recognises your levels and pushes you onto harder levels, the tasks give you options too."* This desire to be pushed to the next level is common among gifted learners. **Jess**'s teacher noted that between the ages of five and seven *"maths problems of any type fulfilled her, as long as I could explain the next level. Games like 'maths baseball' where her team could win really appealed. Her teammates even looked to her for guidance."*

Problem-solving strategies

Gifted children problem-solve differently. **Lucy** said: *"If maths doesn't make sense, I might try reading it a different way; for example reading the last sentence first, in a backwards order'.* Her first-grade teacher recognised her gift: *"she saw patterns easily – she could draw out how she solved the problem for other kids."*

It benefits all students when teachers encourage learners to be explicit and describe how they problem-solve, but this can be challenging for some gifted learners. **Jess** was gifted early at maths. Her teacher, a friend of the family, recalled how she was *"able to connect dots quickly and didn't get distracted by social stuff."* Her mother, also a teacher, agreed: *"from day one, Jess was different to other kids – she was able to focus much earlier. She was into schedules; she wanted her easel on vacation so she could make plans."*

At two years of age, Jess would add people at tables in restaurants. At five, when her mother refused to teach her multiplication, she looked at her mother's whiteboard and figured out how to do it in one night. Despite this, because the answers were 'automatic' in her head, she found it hard to explain how she problem-solved: *"how can I show the work when the answer just appears?"* Backtracking was difficult and inconvenient.

Putting the gifted learner into a tutor role is an interesting challenge for teachers to facilitate. Building on the adage 'to teach is to learn twice', turning the pupil into a tutor makes the brain more agile. By the time Jess got to High School, she had mastered it and, whenever her maths teacher was absent, she requested that Jess teach the class!

Peer learning

Challenge is also essential for **Ava**, aged fifteen. Her favourite subject is maths, because *"I figure out questions really quickly, I just recognise what I have to do."* Her primary teacher spoke about the importance of maths challenges: *"Ava needed something that made her think and work it out."* She sourced an old 'Figure it Out' maths book from her own schooldays to challenge her. She felt it was good to *"get her to explain her own approach and thought process."* This builds learner confidence, expands the learner and enables them to develop a sense of ownership over their learning.

Ava's mother advocates peer-learning to enable pupils to be *"collaborative creative thinkers."* She remarked particularly on *"the recognition Ava needed and received by having the opportunity to help her peers."* When I asked Ava how she would advise teachers to support gifted learners, she replied: *"Maintain their motivation by challenging them with work at their level."*

Focus and planning

Outstanding problem-solving ability can sustain concentration for lengthy periods of time and support drive in gifted learners. For **Sasha**, an affable seventeen-year-old, maths and science were 'her thing'. *"I like to spend time on maths, pursuing the right answer."* Her interest in these subjects provides a strong career motivator for her – *"I got into science at school, and I want to be a doctor. I'm really motivated about solving huge challenges, like cures for diseases."* Her father noticed her 'difference' from a young age, and her private maths tutor described her as a student with extraordinary inner drive, a strong executive function and ability to plan. *"I don't think she has much conception of how bright she is. She comes with the menu for me. I wait for her to ask questions to know where to go next. Sometimes she'll send an advance text, so I know what she wants to study in the next class."*

Clearly rare, this reveals a learner who is metacognitive with the capacity to self-assess – the ability to identify gaps in her own knowledge – leading her to achieve *"four times what an average student would in the same session"*, according to her teacher. It is helpful to be aware of this strong 'planning' facility among gifted learners, and to find ways to optimise it.

Strategic thinking

Ethan, a twenty-three-year-old student of Medicine, has a strong focus and executive function. Science, maths and problem-solving were his 'go to' interests: *"I love the challenge of trying to deal with something I can't grasp right away."* In primary school, he was given maths books for *"years ahead of me – I was flying through them."* His teacher described him as a *"good-humoured boy who loved multi-step maths problems."* She based such problems on his local rural environment. Always keen, he would *"light up at the notion of a new topic in any subject, it was another new challenge."* Independent, too: *"he could fly solo, all I had to do was assign a project to him and he was off."*

In his transition year (at age fifteen to sixteen), Ethan completed a one-week internship in a local hospital. This was the catalyst for him to become a doctor. His drive and focus multiplied. He achieved top grades in his exams. But to do so he knew he had to be strategic – he worked out that the study of English was slowing him down. He approached his teacher to share his concerns, and he was allowed to skip English essays. The outcome was that he won a national scholarship for six years to study medicine.

Strategy was also apparent in his choice of sport – he became a national long-jump champion, something he could excel at independently. Always self-motivated, his mother said: *"Ethan did most things himself – he sorted things out himself, and we took him to whatever he wanted, like athletics."* For Ethan, the *"gifted learner has to help themselves first and aim for a level higher to help your own development."*

Logical thinking

At fifty-eight, **Melissa** is the oldest gifted learner interviewed. Nominated by her maths teacher as the stand-out gifted learner of a forty-two-year career, she describes herself as *"logical to a fault, methodical and impatient – things make sense or they don't."* She relished challenge: *"At the age of ten, when the teacher asked to get the area of a circle, I made it into four squares, I knew it was more than three and less than four – conceptually I could see it. I was almost inventing 'pi' myself without knowing it!"*

She recalled that good teacher methodologies mattered – her teacher *"wallpapered the wall, tiled the floor, he was progressive."* She loved patterns too, a core feature of abstract thinking: *"I still do the Sudoku and crossword every day. I play bridge, it's logic."* Reflecting on her education, she said: *"I probably wasn't challenged enough, repetitive maths frustrated me – just move on."*

Stimulating environments matter

Melissa recalls a stimulating upbringing: *"I was challenged within my family from a young age, so many adults coming and going. My uncle, a doctor, engaged me, getting me to read the newspaper for him."* She chose accountancy as a career because she *"liked the work, the problem-solving, the trouble-shooting and selecting future trainees for the Company"* – all searching activities. She believes it's important that parents and teachers of gifted children *"challenge them educationally and in other ways, for example through reading, maths, projects, running, being timed."*

Her mother was the driver of her education. When she didn't do as well as expected in her mock exams, her mother let her know. Her maths teacher agreed that *"Melissa enjoyed maths; never a frown, she was happy – always near top marks in every test. It was her mother who applied the pressure; she saw that Melissa had a rare talent and wanted her to be challenged."* In response her teacher provided extra work but adds: *"I suppose I could have done more but didn't know how – I was a new teacher myself."*

Reflecting on the current 'Project Maths' initiative in Ireland, her teacher said: *"it would have really suited Melissa – she loved relating to the real world."* That said, Melissa's exceptional talent was clear to her teacher too: *"she was willing to make her learning visible, always engaged at the level of passing on information to others."* This skill transferred into Melissa's work – in her job she mentors trainee accountants.

Innovation

Although **Rhys**, aged sixteen, is cross-talented and excels across the board, maths, science and technology are his favourite subjects: *"I love a hard problem that takes me time to solve."* For a project in technology he was asked to improve and change a wheelchair lift that he designed. Using his problem-solving and creative-thinking skills he *"adapted a pulley lift to a scissors lift"* and *"did a much better project as a result."* In primary school he loved chess and won a national entrepreneurial competition as part of a team of five, designing a board game to combat global warming for children.

Solution focused, Rhys remarked about his entrepreneurial project: "*I probably came up with most of the ideas*" then modestly adds "*but everyone contributed.*" He is self-aware: "*Repetitive, purposeless work frustrates me.*" His mother saw that the activities that fulfilled him were "*problem-solving, competitions and quizzes*" and she fed them to him. She reported that no challenge or "*more of the same*" drains him: "*he needs to be using his brain power.*"

Rhys's teacher discovered that he thrived on research topics – he loved being rewarded with a 'Research Hour', not money. When he had finished his classwork, she allowed him to draw a line under it and write 'my own work'. He could then pick any sum on any page he wanted. Gifted learners have high expectations of their teachers – "*Teachers who didn't go out of their way to make class interesting didn't help me. Teachers should challenge gifted students and encourage them to be creative and independent.*"

Using a 'no limits' approach, Rhys's teacher gave him ownership for his own learning – this "*fulfilled him most of all.*" She added "*bright children like Rhys should be challenged. I always had extension material available.*" Creative and open-ended in her teaching and learning, she pushed the class towards difficult problem-solving and a growth mindset, encouraging 'random thinking', where "*the learner didn't necessarily have to come up with the answer but with reasonable approaches to solving the problem.*" When learners came across a difficult maths question she would say "*I have no idea but let's figure it out together.*" During lockdown she challenged the class to "*make a real chair out of wood and send back a picture of them sitting on it.*" There were no limits to the challenges this teacher offered.

How to help – problem-solving

☞ Challenge is fundamental to the wellbeing of gifted learners. The alternative is boredom, disenchantment and dissatisfaction. Respond to their innate thirst with complex, multi-step, layered problems.

☞ Give gifted learners responsibility for individual projects, along with opportunities to play team games to build social skills and credibility. Balance intellectual challenge with their still being a child.

☞ With maths, pre-assess the student and provide challenges at their level, not the class level. Give them access to pattern work, matrices and programs such as 'Mathletics' where they can move onto harder work at their own pace. Remember they are asynchronous learners.

☞ Create opportunities for gifted learners to play with maths and devise ways to solve a problem. Allow them to share their method and see if it resonates with others. A peer tutor role will challenge them to find ways to explain how to solve a problem, maintaining motivation.

☞ Develop the learner's planning and executive skills by promoting self-assessment. Encourage them to take the lead in their teaching and learning by coming up with their own questions and learning plan.

☞ Good teacher methodologies matter and are noticed by gifted learners. Facilitate hands-on activities so they discover how to solve a problem. They particularly love real-life application.

☞ Encourage them to enter quizzes, crossword competitions and chess matches to fine-tune their skills, give them access to a wider pool of competition and build confidence through outside validation.

☞ Ask them to talk about their problem-solving strategies and draw them out if they find it difficult to articulate. This develops metacognition.

☞ Create a 'we're all learners together' culture to enable learners to think for themselves and to value their own diverse contributions.

Chapter 7: Avid reading

Learning to read is one area that parents, caregivers and teachers of gifted learners generally don't have to worry about. Thanks to their superior brain development, it tends to come easily to them. Most tend to be very good readers, with some acquiring the skill very early and a large majority going onto be avid readers, absorbing books well beyond their years.

> **Key Point**
>
> Most gifted learners tend to be very good readers, with some acquiring the skill very early and a large majority going onto be avid readers.

Sometimes, however, keeping the gifted reader challenged is hard, borne out by the fact that some of our gifted learners become bored in class. Still, such a pattern can be avoided if we identify gifted learners and support them with the same interest and resourcing that we provide for struggling learners. We need to keep their curiosity and learning spark alive by challenging and engaging them from the beginning. Providing interesting reading material at their level is key.

Gifted learners have been characterised as individuals who read voraciously, perform well above their grade levels, possess advanced vocabularies and do well in tests.[37] They usually demonstrate advanced language abilities in comparison with children of the same age. They use words easily, accurately and creatively in new and innovative contexts, and speak in semantically and syntactically complex sentences.[38] The interviews conducted for this book bear out these findings, and also suggest that a further hallmark of gifted learners might be an early, obvious love of books. For example **Ruby**, now twenty-four, recalled *"hiding in the bookshelves"* as a small child.

Brain development and learning to read

It is often taken for granted that children learn to read; however, learning to read is a skill that must be taught.[39] Not only does it have to be taught; the child's brain must be sufficiently developed before a child can learn

---

[37] Vacca, J.A.L., Vacca, R.T. & Gove, M.K. (1991) *Instructor's Manual to Accompany Reading and Learning to Read*. HarperCollins.

[38] Bond, C.F. & Titus, L.J. (1983) Social facilitation: A meta-analysis of 241 studies. *Psychological Bulletin*, 94(2), 265-292.

[39] Seidenberg, M.S. (2013) The Science of Reading and Its Educational Implications. *Language Learning and Development*, 9(4), 331–360.

the skill. While a child can be helped to memorise words, until their brain is adequately developed they are not going to be able to read.[40] And unless a child's brain has matured sufficiently, they won't be able to read fluently. Fluent reading requires much more than a good memory – it requires the ability to comprehend the meanings of words, sentences, paragraphs, the whole story. In essence, it requires cognitive and affective development.

In Chapter 3, we examined Renzulli's three-ring model of giftedness. The gifted reader evidences the three aspects of giftedness that Renzulli proposes – above-average ability, task commitment and creativity – in the area of reading.[41] Both cognitive and affective behaviours of gifted readers may be explained within the framework of Renzulli's three rings.

Let's not underestimate what is involved in learning to read; it can be a difficult skill to master even when it is being formally taught. Some children have a hard time reaching fluency even by the time they are eight or nine years old. If a child reaches fluency before the age of five having been taught to read then there's a good chance the child is quite advanced, since the brain must have reached a sufficient level of maturity. However, where a child teaches him- or herself to read without any formal instruction at all, there is no question about their giftedness.[42]

A self-taught reader is a child who has figured out how to read without any formal reading instruction, thereby 'breaking the code'. Self-taught readers figure out the symbol system on their own, sometimes with little more than a video about the alphabet or simply being read to frequently.[43] This is extraordinary. But being read to frequently is not to be under-estimated: it develops the voice in the child's head, boosts their motivation for reading and shows them that words on a page convey meaning – fulfilling one of the most innate human needs of all, the desire for story.

The acquisition of early reading was a frequent theme of the case study interviews. **Olga**, now twenty and a student of global commerce and languages, was observed reading a broadsheet newspaper as young as three years old. Her mother recalls: *"She taught herself to read. Books and reading were a big part of home, bedtime stories were like a religion."* Olga agrees: *"I always had my head in a book."* Her teachers made a

---

40 Brown, T.T. (2012) *Brain Development During the Preschool Years*. SpringerLink [online].
41 Vosslamber, A. (2002) Gifted Readers: Who Are They, and How Can They Be Served in the Classroom? *Gifted Child Today*, 25(2), 14-20.
42 Bainbridge, C. (2020) *Are Children Gifted If They Learn How to Read Earlier Than Others?* Verywell Family [online].
43 Bainbridge, C. (2021) *How Learning to Read Without Instruction Relates to Giftedness*. Verywell Family [online].

difference: *"I had a great teacher when I was nine years old – she gave me novels and books to read, extra activities to challenge me."* Her teacher described Olga as a child whose *"reading stood out, a voracious reader who read organically. It was vital that I exposed her to a broad range of reading."* Her love of reading translated into writing and creativity: *"When I was eleven I wrote a short story, and my teacher rated it at a fifteen year-old standard."*

Becoming an avid reader

It is fascinating to consider how gifted learners become 'avid readers.' Twelve-year-old **Dylan** – an intense, musically-gifted boy – showed early interest in reading. He could read music at the age of four – his mother said *"the staff, note values and rhythm came easily to him. By age five he was pursuing his own books."* Books were a welcome distraction at school: *"I would bring books into school and read through breaks, during class, they kept me out of trouble."* By eleven, he was reading eight-hundred-page books on holiday. His teacher noticed his appetite for different sorts of books – including history, mythology and science – and saw the need to *"let him engage in holistic topics that interested him."*

Sabrina's mother reported that she would read stories to her daughter at two years of age to get her to sleep. *"She wanted me to read four books, and she'd notice if I skipped a word."* At primary school, she *"went through books like crazy."* Now fifteen and linguistically strong, Sabrina reads less than she once did. This pattern was noted among a number of gifted learners interviewed, a factor that the exam system has to answer for. Still, her mother credits Sabrina's interest in reading as a strong influencer of her creative writing: *"She recently wrote a poem in response to a painting from the point of view of a doll thrown away by a child, whereas all the other students wrote from the point of view of the child."*

Emma, now nineteen and a university student studying Criminology, says *"I always had my nose stuck in a book."* Her enjoyment of reading helped her with her preferred course and career choice: *"I loved reading history and English, a skill vital for reading law books."*

Lucy, eleven, was *"reading the Harry Potter books by the time she was seven years old."* Her mother said she absorbed books *"well beyond her years"*, although because Lucy had extreme sensory issues she couldn't take her to a library as a young child – the high ceilings and low vibrations meant *"she was hearing stuff nobody else could hear."* Parents of gifted learners have little choice but to work around challenges like these. When Lucy was seven, her teacher saw that reading and writing *"fulfilled her"*, particularly *"when she was allowed to express herself in her own way."* Diary entry activities based on picture books extended her, and her teacher showed her how to craft a 'double-entry' journal whereby she would select a page or part of a book and then examine it from different perspectives.

Bloom's Taxonomy

Bloom's Taxonomy (see figure 7.1) describes the depth of understanding a student has as they progress through learning content.[44] In this model, the highest levels of critical thinking are 'analysis', 'evaluation' and 'creation'. We need to be operating at those levels as often as possible with our gifted learners.[45] This means asking more probing questions when we talk about what they are reading, and being flexible when we seek to encourage creativity – especially as some gifted learners can find writing challenging. For example, teachers can set assignments such as a letter to the author, journaling and free writing on a topic of the learner's own choice.

The taxonomy is a useful teaching aid to keep close at hand for easy reference by teacher and student. The gifted learner can evaluate their own performance against it, for example by becoming aware that when they connect ideas they are 'analysing', when they justify their stance on something they are 'evaluating', and when they design new or original work they are 'creating' and operating at the highest level of the taxonomy. This provides useful feedback for the gifted reader.

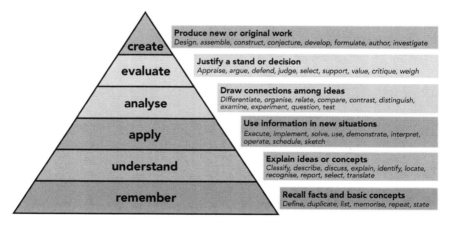

Figure 7.1: Bloom's Taxonomy

---

44   Bloom, B.S. (1956) *Taxonomy of educational objectives*. David McKay.
45   O'Neal, E. (2017). *Got a gifted reader? Here are an educator's top tips for story time*. Pick Any Two [online].

The QUEST approach

When reading with a child, use the QUEST approach to facilitate critical and creative reading.[46]

- **Q** = Use high-level **Q**uestioning
- **U** = When possible, level **U**p
- **E** = **E**nrich the child's life with subject matter
- **S** = Know the child's learning **S**trengths
- **T** = Use **T**echnology to the child's advantage

Q = Use high-level Questioning

With our gifted learners, we need to exercise their thinking at a higher order level. Examples of simple and higher order questions are shown in figure 7.2.

Rather than asking…	Ask this instead.
What happened in this chapter?	How do you feel about what happened in this chapter? (evaluation)
Describe the character.	Is this character a good person? (evaluation)
Why did x happen?	What events could have predicted that x would happen? (synthesis)
Can you read another chapter?	What do you think will happen in the next chapter? (synthesis)
Can you write the next chapter?	Write about how the main character will respond to x event in the next chapter. (creation)

Figure 7.2: higher order questions (adapted from O'Neal, 2017)

U = Move Up a level

Two avenues available to meet the needs of gifted readers in the classroom are reading acceleration and individual enrichment.[46] Acceleration means grouping learners by ability rather than age. It can happen within a class by facilitating the gifted child to read ahead at their level individually, or in a reading/discussion group where the other children may be at a similar level. Grouping students by ability for reading

---

46 Johnson, D.W., & Johnson, R.T. (1987). *Learning together and alone: Cooperative, competitive, and individualistic learning*, 2nd ed (pp. xiii, 193). Prentice-Hall.

instruction has been found to increase understanding and appreciation of literature,[47] although some of the interviewed teachers disagreed with this approach since we live in a 'mixed-ability world'. Still, having a wide variety of levelled books and access to technology is essential. 'Accelerated Reader' is a popular computer-based reading resource for this purpose, and it can be accessed at home too.

E = Enrich the child's life with subject matter

Children's varied interests should be cultivated. When we are interested in something we want more of it. This can work for a book or subject your child adores. Listen to music with similar themes, cook food from the storyline or the setting, use drama to mirror the characters, or make up science experiments to replicate events in the plot. We do this when our children are little, and we can continue it when they are older – gifted learners benefit from hands-on experiences.

S = Know the child's learning Strengths

Today we have increased awareness about how we learn best. Helping a gifted learner to figure out how they learn best makes them more self-aware. Do they have learning preferences? Are they more suited to learning presented through auditory, verbal, visual, intuitive or kinaesthetic channels or a combination? Or to put it more simply, when information is presented in that way, does it makes learning easier and more fun? Listening to books, bringing in guest speakers, acting out scenes, linking books to TV or movies and creating hands-on projects to evaluate plot devices are exciting ways to create meaningful literacy activities for gifted learners.

T = Use Technology to the child's advantage

Use technology to access levels of learning that the child wouldn't otherwise experience. The interviews conducted for this book showed that gifted learners love to be pushed onto harder levels, and technology facilitates this. The key with technology is to participate with the child, to use it in moderation and not to rely exclusively on it. Our children are preparing for lives that will be embedded with more technology than ours, and we need to embrace the idea that they will be learning differently than we do if we want to successfully support them on that journey.

---

[47] Sakiey, E. (1980). *Reading for the Gifted: Instructional Strategies Based on Research.* ERIC [online].

How to help – avid reading

Strategies for parents and caregivers:

☞ Read to your child every day, the earlier the better to develop the language centre of the brain. This helps the early brain to develop and mature. Give books as gifts and encourage others to do so too.

☞ Make reading a pleasurable shared activity that is enjoyed as much as any game. Play with words and ideas. We develop readers by reading. It makes the young reader want to emulate us.

☞ Join the library with your child and make it a weekly visit if possible. Encourage them to choose their own books. Browse different kinds of books and notice where their interests lie.

☞ Discuss the craft, decision-making and point of view of different authors – this helps children to see other perspectives, something that gifted learners sometimes have difficulty with.

Strategies for teachers and schools:

☞ Challenging materials should be made available to gifted readers. Introduce a wide variety of reading genres so they see the different ways that authors communicate through fact and fiction.

☞ Build excitement for reading through paired reading with children from other classes – big buddy, little buddy is always a winner!

☞ Challenge gifted learners' reading comprehension by encouraging them to use quotations and evidence to support their answers. I refer to this as PQAR and recommend it as an exam strategy:

- **P** = make your point
- **Q** = support it with a quotation or evidence
- **A** = analyse and discuss your point, connecting ideas
- **R** = keep your answer tight by reflecting on and referring back to the question

☞ Enhance the creativity of gifted learners by focusing on their descriptive powers – for example by writing descriptions for a particular setting using each of the five senses.

☞ Use Bloom's Taxonomy as a means to help gifted readers with self-evaluation. Use QUEST as a way to develop critical, creative readers.

Chapter 8: Quick learning

Gifted learners understand readily, learn quickly and retain what is learned. They frequently pick up new skills without the need for repetition. However, this doesn't mean that they don't need to be taught. They still need to be introduced to new concepts, and often need direct instruction. Some areas are particularly challenging for them; for example, the gifted eight- and nine-year-olds that I teach do not automatically know how to write fluently.

> **Key Point**
>
> *Gifted learners understand readily, learn quickly and retain what is learned. However, this doesn't mean that they don't need to be taught.*

Quick learning – essentially advanced learning – was a notable feature of each of the gifted learners interviewed for this book. Despite their genius, however, there was a clear demand among them to be understood and validated personally, to be 'seen' for the type of learners they are. In teachers' and parents' eyes, gifted learners demand and are demanding. This chapter explores how to better understand and enhance their quick learning gift.

Single-mindedness

Amy, aged fifteen, always found learning easy: she describes herself as an *"academic person with a photographic memory."* She loves science *"it gets my brain working."* As a result of a family move, she changed countries and schools and in doing so skipped a year level at age twelve: *"The transition of school and country was a big jump, but I enjoyed it and adjusted quickly. I started French and German and although my classmates had one year done already, I felt I was learning more."* It should be noted here that while skipping a year worked well for Amy, adjustment and self-esteem issues may arise and it should be approached with caution. Attending a more advanced class on a trial basis is usually a better strategy.

Her mother describes Amy as *"intelligent, original, not interested in copying others but interested in the idea that others learn 'another way'."* She is aware of different ways to learn and interested in learning itself. *"Amy is very serious, she goes off and studies on her own for hours and hours; this can exhaust her at times, and I have to remind her to take breaks."* Concerned about poor standards, *"she wants the teacher to stay on task and doesn't need to know the teacher or the children's names."*

Demanding in her pursuit of learning, Amy is intolerant of timewasters, poor work or lack of preparedness. *"She reported a teacher to the Year Head for not teaching well enough."* When I expressed surprise at this, neither Amy nor her mother had any difficulty with it. This is a reminder that some gifted learners can be quite matter-of-fact and emotionless at times. Such instances are also teachable moments that offer an opportunity to show the value of empathy and walking in another's shoes.

Independent learning

Maria, forty-two, an electronic engineer, found learning very easy and *"understood content first time round at school. I loved maths, physics, accounting and learning languages. I was always top of the class without any effort, but I wasn't challenged. I loved to work things out. One teacher gave me extra maths work; it was okay but not enough."* Her problem-solving abilities transferred into the workplace: *"At work when others have difficulty understanding a concept, I diagram it to make it clear."*

Her mother noticed her eldest child's talent from an early age: *"she adored jigsaws, they were so easy for her that we turned them upside down so she couldn't see the pictures. She absolutely loved tests and getting things right. With reading, she had a few library cards on the go!"* Reflecting on her gifted daughter, her mother said: *"it's good that learning was easy for her because the rest was difficult; she was a sensitive soul and found the interpersonal challenging."* Social and emotional difficulties are explored in Part 5.

As competent as Maria was, she felt that she wasn't *"shown how to study, to become an independent learner. I didn't feel I reached my potential in university. I didn't have the self-discipline, I relied on cramming."* This has had a considerable impact on Maria's self-esteem: *"I'm still traumatised that I didn't get a first-class honour because I should have, it's a difficult way to live. While objectively I did well, I felt like a failure."* Her utter dismay is tangible, tinged with resentment that educators hadn't provided her with better career guidance: *"There is a gap in the system – when I didn't know what I wanted to do, I wasn't helped to figure out what that was. Guidance was subject-based, presuming high exam results equals Medicine, instead of looking at what career would fulfil me as a person."*

Mindset and memorisation

Ruby, aged twenty-four, displayed an early grasp of 'underlying principles' when learning: *"Learning tables, in primary school, I tried to come up with patterns and hidden systems to explain to other children."* Her Reception teacher agreed: *"her thought process was advanced, and she understood* *the needs of the teacher almost as a peer."* This capacity continued as she moved through school: *"In any subject I was able to come up with mnemonics immediately to aid understanding and help me remember."*

Ruby draws on her musical acumen to learn cognitive tasks that require a particular mindset: *"I usually have a melody or song that I associate with different levels of task difficulty or intensity depending on the level of concentration required. For exams, performances and general psyching myself up, I refer to this music in my head and it regulates me to the correct level for the performance. Now I just do it unconsciously for stimulation."*

This skill was an advantage for content-based learning but *"my creative giftedness didn't shine through as much in secondary because memorising was over-emphasised."* The habitual emphasis on memory work presented a challenge for her in university, where she had to learn to adjust to *"critical analysis over remembering."* Nevertheless, being seen and heard at all levels of her education benefited Ruby's development. *"Teachers believed in me, I got satisfaction and grew from their allowing me to ask additional questions."*

Relating to real life

Miguel, aged forty and a paediatrician, found learning easy from the start. His mother described him as *"always curious and anxious to know new things even when very small."* Endowed with a strong work ethic, he got a *"great sense of satisfaction on task completion"*, which has become a feature of his life. His teacher described a boy with an *"independence and sense of self-containment, not bothered by others."* He had a *"pep in his step"* when he was *"onto something new, learning a new concept – especially maths,"* where *"he was way ahead of others."*

Speaking with Miguel, he said he was fortunate to have a strong long-term memory and a *"healthy brain."* He explained he *"never crammed"* for an exam. More challenged in secondary school, he had a flair for learning languages and was particularly drawn to maths and science. At university he found he had a strength for anatomy because *"I could visualise it"* and went onto win a national award in the subject. He loved it when the lecturer/surgeon showed that learning had a *"real-life purpose."*

Miguel describes his learning style as *"quite visual with a photographic memory."* A problem-solver, maths for him was *"like a diagnosis to be made."* When he studied, he got a *"strong sense"* of what he was learning. His problem-solving style transferred into his work: *"I am immediately engaged by a problem as a paediatrician – kids would have seen umpteen doctors before me."* Teacher integrity was important to him – having had excellent and *"not so good"* teachers, he had no time for those who were 'bluffing' – *"I really admired teachers who would say 'I don't know'."*

Miguel was sporty and athletic at school too. His mother was concerned about his *"balance of time"* given his desire to study medicine in his final year. Reflecting now, she feels that his athletic, competitive nature helped with his studies. Drawing analogies between study and sport, Miguel's attitude towards exams is revealing: *"when academia is what you do, your exams are your Cup Final – the day to show off your knowledge and skill."*

Balancing dedication and perfectionism

Ava, aged fifteen, was described by her primary school teacher as *"exceptional."* Her mother noticed this early: *"Ava gives her all – she has overcome many challenges including open-heart surgery as a baby and more surgery as a toddler. From the outset, teachers were astounded with her ability; her book work was outstanding. She always wanted a head-start on learning what was coming next, from the time she was four years of age."*

Ava says she extends herself: *"In Science I might think of something that isn't written in the book, but I want to know for myself. In algebra I would think of different ways, then evaluate the quickest option."* An evaluative learner, she likes it when *"teachers tell students how to improve – I apply their feedback to myself."* She likes to know there are other learners like herself: *"I like having a peer to talk with and relate to at the same level."*

Her teacher said: *"I put differentiation in place to challenge Ava. Maths made her think and work it out. Mind maps allowed her to be creative and intellectual simultaneously."* From an early age, her teacher encouraged her to practice self-assessment using SALF (Self-Assessment and Learning Folders).[48] There, she noticed that Ava could be very hard on herself.

The same high standard applied to *"homework – it had to be meticulous."* By the age of twelve, Ava was spending two-and-a-half hours per evening on her homework. On a half-day from school she had already spent four hours on it. Her advanced learning took on another dimension – her mother said her perfectionism impacted on family time. Ava admitted *"I do study a lot and may put in more effort than most, I want to see myself do well. I expect it of myself."* Perfectionism is discussed in detail in Chapter 18.

---

48   O'Mahoney, A. & Ryan, R.M.C. (2018) *SALF: Self-Assessment and Learning Folders*. Outside the Box Learning Resources.

Engagement and fulfilment

Dylan, aged twelve, is a multifaceted boy who doesn't suffer fools easily: *"I don't enjoy school that much, but it is important for a competitive society."* His teacher would regularly have to say *"I'll have to look it up"* in response to his questions. A quick learner with an *"outstanding intellect"*, his learning could be *"interest-dependent"* and he might *"only listen for a short period of time."* The exception was music – *"it brought him into a different zone."*

Dylan was strong orally and processed fast – there was no time-wasting, but writing frustrated him *"He resisted pen to paper; his mind was working too fast to transfer it to paper."* He sees subtle relationships across topics but *"always wants proof"* and *"would seek out multiple viewpoints."* His mother agreed: *"He won't take face value, he will see the subtleties"* – a sign of giftedness.[30] He feels fulfilled as a learner when he's *"satisfied that I've learned something, solidified and confirmed it, especially something I've been wondering about for ages."* His teacher concurs – with the 'science blast', he was fulfilled: *"he created an electric car using the tools given with supporting PowerPoints."* His teacher counselled *"it is important to give him a choice of topics and opportunities to engage him."*

His mother is adamant that *"we should really see the gifted learner for who they are."* She recognised Dylan's strengths and limitations – for example, his ability to *"visualise what he wants to create and follow through to the letter of the law"*. However, she said it comes with a price – *"if it doesn't work out, he can lose the plot."* Repetitive work such as writing sentences or completing multiple maths problems of the same nature greatly frustrate him. He is *"the most demanding"* of her three children, and she has to be *"one step ahead of him"* – providing reassurance, a listening ear and validation.

How to help – quick learning

Strategies for parents and caregivers:

☞ Give gifted learners puzzles early – jigsaws, sudoku and crosswords of increasing difficulty. Chess, brain, mind and memory games can give gifted learners lots of satisfaction.

☞ Gifted learners are exacting. If you don't know something, it is best to say: "I don't know" or "I'll have to check it out." Gifted learners admire the truth, and it makes for a better relationship.

☞ Watch the tendency of gifted learners to overdo it, for example with homework, and give them advice in this regard. Explain how their brain needs a break from time to time to assimilate learning.

☞ For years gifted learners have tuned out as a coping skill! Help them develop their listening skills by listening to audiobooks, tuning in for directions or sharing something they heard another pupil say.

☞ Because gifted learners have high standards and high expectations of themselves, they can be touchy and fragile when studying. Watch their mood coming up to exams, and monitor nutrition, rest and relaxation.

☞ Be aware that gifted learners can test your patience! Be ready for it and connect, where possible, with their underlying frustration.

Strategies for teachers and schools:

☞ Provide a space for challenge and growth. Gifted learners like being tested, but most of all they crave formative feedback that is relevant to them. Notice their strengths and help them to build on them.

☞ We can wrongly assume that gifted learners know how to study effectively. Study skills such as goal-setting and note-taking help them take control of their own learning and are of lifelong benefit.

☞ Gifted learners need more validation than most, so show that you believe in them. Because they generally perform at the top of the class, we may underestimate how much personal affirmation matters.

☞ Challenge gifted learners to evaluate their own learning and devise systems to explain their thinking to the class. Notice how they draw on visual, auditory, verbal, intuitive and/or kinaesthetic channels.

☞ Show purpose and applications for learning. Gifted learners love real-world relevance. Likewise, encourage them to show how their outside interests can give them a perspective, for example at exam time.

☞ Provide them with a differentiated plan of work – they appreciate it. Repetitive tasks or more of the same is not what they want.

Part 3: Creativity

Chapter 9: Cognitive flexibility

Cognitive flexibility is a mindset and skill that all learners should be exposed to, but it will be particularly welcomed by the creative, gifted learner who is naturally inclined in that direction. Most problem-solving requires our brains to retrieve memories and information of personal experiences, knowledge, and creativity to address a task at hand. How well we do this depends on how 'flexibly' we can navigate these areas to overcome obstacles, learn from past mistakes and process new information. Cognitive flexibility ensures that we don't end up stuck in a situation in which we are immobilised and can't move forward.

> ## Key Point
> Cognitive flexibility ensures that we don't end up stuck in a situation in which we are immobilised and can't move forward.

From a learning perspective cognitive flexibility, and more broadly the ability to think flexibly, allows us to analyse a situation, and figure out a plan and solution(s) by changing the way we think, accepting other perspectives and adapting to new and unexpected variables. It lets us shift between challenges to manage complex problems, make sense, organise information, make connections, ask questions and decide what to do next.

Flexible and divergent ways of thinking

Gifted children are often flexible thinkers who use different alternatives and approaches to problem solving. **Ava**, aged fifteen, enjoyed flexible thinking and *"considering problems from a number of viewpoints"* across subject areas: *"In atoms there are four shells; I would want to know what more there is to this, such as the rings of Saturn."* In maths she used both divergent and convergent thinking to arrive at solutions: *"In algebra I would think of different ways to perform it, then evaluate the best way."*

Emma, now nineteen and studying Law and Criminology, would appear to have selected the ideal course to facilitate justice and fairness in her future career. Her mother described how her daughter showed flexibility in thinking; she recalled her history teacher reporting that Emma practised a style where *"she would sit back, weigh up a topic, assess it and then offer her view."* Invariably, she said, *"she would hit the nail on the head."* This is a good example of Emma employing more than one thinking approach to examine evidence, then evaluate the situation and draw her conclusion. Her German teacher said her work showed *"a different way of* *looking at things"*, leading her to *"frame her answers with expression and imagination. She was able to put everything into perspective."*

Rhys, fifteen, typifies cognitive flexibility – a young man with a flexible mind who can turn his hand to anything. Rhys loves to consider all the options, act on his decision and make or produce as a result. His life to date is full of achievements arising from the application of his finely tuned mind, intellect and perspective. From technology to chess, and from playing the flute to national athletics relays, there is little that Rhys doesn't succeed at when he applies himself. When I asked his teacher about him, she said: *"He was always open to learning."* This open-mindedness is a key facet of cognitive flexibility.

Ava, Emma and Rhys's cases support Jennifer Katz's contention that students who are gifted are most often divergent thinkers, meaning that multiple areas of the brain are involved in their thinking.[49] This results in lateral, connective thought patterns rather than a convergent, logical-sequential processing style. Gifted learners demonstrate an ability to think abstractly and grasp concepts much better than their peers.[50] They have exceptional problem-solving abilities and can conceive higher-order relations. Moreover, they have a need for precision and an ability to perceive many sides of a question by thinking metaphorically and visualising models and systems.

Logical thinking and intolerance

Gifted learners have logical imperatives related to their complex thought patterns – they expect the world to make sense. This can lead them to argue extensively, correct errors, and strive for precision of thought in every endeavour. **Dylan**, aged twelve, is a case in point. He fits the profile of a flexible, divergent thinker with a twist. An intriguing boy, he loves *"big picture thinking"* and considering multiple possibilities for ideas and problems. Before he entered his final year in primary school, he was *"a bit concerned"*, so he asked many people what it would be like before reaching the conclusion that it would be *"a breeze."*

However, as his mother explains, Dylan can sometimes take his quest for knowledge to extremes, to his detriment in the classroom – especially with classmates. He *"persists with questioning, sometimes showing off superior knowledge, to the exclusion of others."* His teacher confirmed that *"he might only see things his way"* and can have a *"short tolerance of other learners' needs."* Argumentative by nature, motivated by justice and the pursuit of

---

49 Katz, J. (2013) *UDL & Gifted Education: Who Are Gifted Learners?* [online].
50 Oak Crest Academy (2018) *11 Ways Gifted Students Learn Differently* [online]

proof, Dylan has found himself frequently misunderstood and excluded at school, which has also had repercussions at home. He typifies the gifted learner who requires careful individual mediation by both teacher and parent.

Pattern recognition

Pattern recognition is the ability to see order in chaos and find solutions to complex problems. Pattern recognition helps us make predictions and educated guesses based on our observations, and leads to discovering a new understanding, a new path forward. Understanding patterns helps us see relationships and develop broader views of complex concepts and operations. Finding patterns is done by breaking down a complex problem into smaller pieces to help find and better understand any similarities or common elements that problems share. Pattern recognition is also known as computational thinking in the field of computer science.

Ava's performances in and out of school demonstrate pattern recognition and the visualisation of models and systems. Described by her mother as *"the queen of patterns"*, by the age of fifteen she had already won seven out of eleven national titles in Taekwondo. Pattern recognition was evident on the football field and in her dancing too, when her mother recognised the characteristic 'sensitivity and finesse in rhythm, movement and body control' listed in the 'Creativity' section of the GLF. Her teacher agreed that the patterning, breathing and finesse involved in the solo activity of Taekwondo helped Ava to excel at self-expression. She carried this finesse into her classwork, through mind-mapping where she was *"creatively stimulated."*

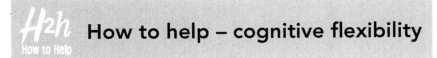

How to help – cognitive flexibility

Strategies for parents and caregivers:

☞ Expose your child to new experiences, cultures and ways of doing things. Take them on trips and expand their circle by introducing them to people from different backgrounds. Build their cognitive flexibility by setting them the task of learning something new.

☞ Elements of cognitive flexibility and divergent thinking can be seen in child's play, for example when preschool children turn cardboard boxes into forts or spaceships. Encourage this – the enthusiastic, open-minded and unconstrained ways in which young children play allow their discovery of ideas to develop and evolve.

☞ Encourage thinking in unconventional ways – ask the child if there could be another way to approach something and introduce 'what if?' scenarios to practise divergent thinking. Help them learn that there could be more than one 'right' way of looking at things.

☞ Challenging a narrative in the media can provide gifted learners with subjects for debate that will require flexible thinking. Always encourage contrarian views to be expressed in a respectful way to help young people see topics from multiple viewpoints.

☞ Practise open-mindedness and ask your child to remind you if you're being 'close-minded'. Open-minded people are more inclusive in their thinking and have a higher curiosity level. When your mind is open you are open to new ideas, and you change what and how you think.

Strategies for teachers and educators:

☞ Practise divergent thinking with your gifted learners as a means to identify opportunities, address difficult problems and challenge the status quo. Use brainstorming, spiderweb diagrams or mind-mapping to encourage them to look at issues from different perspectives.

☞ Excite learners by asking them to repurpose and reengineer some existing resources to show how much can be done with what they already have. Ask them to work in pairs or small groups, and to use divergent thinking to brainstorm before constructing their 'new' item.

☞ Show learners that understanding and being able to identify recurring patterns allows us to make educated guesses and helps us develop the skills of systems thinking and non-linear logic. Pattern recognition also helps with sorting, categorising and building libraries in the brain.

☞ If you're asking the same questions and not getting the results you're looking for, adjust your lens and ask different questions. Shifting the lens from desirability to feasibility, for example, offers a different perspective because the questions you ask will be different.

☞ Show learners how to increase understanding by thinking around an issue to find that 'lightbulb' moment. Exploring 'outside the box' can frighten some learners, but rarely the creative gifted learner.

Chapter 10: Language usage

Many of the gifted learners interviewed for this book showed an early and advanced facility in their use of spoken and written language. Actually, it regularly becomes obvious to parents and teachers that a gifted child is different from his or her siblings and/or peers when observing their language usage – their thirst for language, their word play and their power of self-expression.

> *Key Point*
>
> *It regularly becomes obvious to parents and teachers that a gifted child is different from siblings and/or peers when observing their language usage.*

This chapter looks at the gifted learner's oral and written language capacity. We explored reading in Chapter 7. This is not to suggest that reading should be considered separate from oral and written language; on the contrary, a key recommendation is that oral language, reading and writing should be linked. Good language programmes provide learners with opportunities for speaking, listening, questioning, feeding back, reading and writing.[51]

Early language development

Gifted children learn earlier than their peers. Research with children whose IQ is above 180 has shown that these children develop much earlier than others with regard to their talking, reading and imagination.[52] Carol Bainbridge says that one characteristic of gifted children is advanced language ability.[46] They tend to talk earlier, have larger vocabularies, and use longer sentences than non-gifted children. While most children say their first word at around one year of age, gifted children may begin speaking when they are just nine months old. Some parents even report that their children said their first word as early as six months.

We have seen that as a two-year-old **Sabrina** *"would want four books and she'd notice if I skipped a word"*, indicating early attention to language.

Still, not all gifted children speak early. In fact, some gifted children are late talkers, not talking until they are two years old or more. However, when they do speak, they sometimes skip over typical stages of language development and may begin speaking in full sentences.

---

51 Colangelo, N. & Davis, G.A. (2002) *Handbook on Gifted Education*, 3rd ed. Allyn & Bacon

Jess had an exceptional early facility for language and learning that was noticed by both her parents and teachers. So much so that the gifted programme at her school was set up specially to accommodate her. Unusually, the gifted teacher was also a friend of Jess's mother, and visited when she was a baby in the hospital: *"As a new-born, Jess was staring at my mouth. She was completely focused – laser-focused – on my speaking to her. It was as if the shape of the sound fascinated her, like how I could make noise."* Jess was an early talker and by the age of five was relating to her mother in a manner beyond her years: *"I had really good conversations with her about her day. She related almost adult-like."*

Indicators of advanced language development

In their second year of life, most children increase their vocabulary to about three hundred words. Gifted children, however, will have a larger working vocabulary, approaching that of a four-year-old or older. Advanced vocabulary can refer to the number or the types of words that a child uses.

Typically, the first words a child learns will be nouns: 'mama', 'dada', 'dog', 'ball', 'shop' and so on. Then simple verbs are added, for example 'want', 'go', 'see', 'give'. Gifted children, however, will add connecting words such as 'and' or 'because'. By the age of three, a gifted child's language may resemble adult speech with transitional words such as 'however' or multisyllabic words like 'appropriate'. They may also use time markers, like 'now', 'later', 'first' and 'then', which, along with their advanced vocabulary and more complete sentences, allow them to carry on full conversations with adults.

As a primary student, **Jess** continued to love learning. She recalled a teacher challenging her as a nine-year-old by differentiating spelling to suit her: *"He gave me different words on top of the base list. He would use a dictionary to look up words and sometimes picked words that described me such as 'effervescent' and 'vivacious'"*. This attention affirmed her as a child.

Language development and innate gifts

Advanced language competency can be heavily influenced by innate gifts. **Jude**, aged twelve, attended a stage class and loved theatre from the age of five. Now a professional child actor, he has an exceptional capacity for language, music and drama. *"I'm very good at learning lines for major parts in shows and I love it"*, he admits. *"'Caroline, or Change' was my* *first big show; I'm almost in every scene."* Highly motivated, he says: *"I got the lines one month in advance and learned them every night"*. He is also acutely aware of his own development: *"I notice that my articulation, description and presentation of a character has improved."*

Ruby, twenty-four, displayed a superior quality and quantity of spoken vocabulary and language usage at an early age. Gifted musically, she was able to whistle in tune by the age of two. Her mother explained that she arrived at speaking through singing: *"She was able to sing a complete song before speaking complete sentences. Language and melody intertwine, and the melody seemed to carry the vocabulary."*

Olga's mother recalls being "dumb-founded" when she noticed her baby *"humming along in tune to 'Twinkle Twinkle Little Star' at eight months."* By the age of eleven, Olga was demonstrating a superior quality of writing and *"exceptional imagination."* At the age of ten she won an adjudicated drama competition for a funny sketch that she and her friend composed independently. She was mature and empathic too: *"I could always talk to Olga about my work"*, said her mother. Linguistically strong, Olga is now a student of Global Business, fluent in French and Irish, and learning Spanish.

The importance of vocabulary development

Vocabulary development matters, even for gifted children who may demonstrate strong word knowledge. It should not be ignored. When picturing the gifted student and their thirst for advanced knowledge, it's easy to see how beneficial it is to teach them new vocabulary. Learning about and playing with language is often something that gifted children really enjoy doing.[52] If in doubt, here are some of the key benefits:[53]

- Vocabulary improves reading comprehension. Improving vocabulary skills will also improve understanding of novels and textbooks.
- Vocabulary enhances language development. Children with a rich vocabulary tend to be deeper thinkers, express themselves better and read more, leading to more success academically and communicatively.

---

52 Snyder, J. (2018) *Teaching Vocabulary to Gifted and Advanced Learners—Instructional Strategies that Work*. Soaring with Snyder [online].
53 Seifert, D. (2016) *Top 5 Reasons why Vocabulary Matters*. InferCabulary [online].

- Successful communication or 'saying what you mean' depends upon a good vocabulary. Quite simply, using the right words when talking makes you a more effective communicator.
- Expressing yourself in writing. Having a good vocabulary can help you write more effectively. Students need to use a more formal tone when writing – not conversational language – and to do that, they need a richer vocabulary to tap into words that we don't use when we speak.
- Vocabulary can influence occupational success. The pioneering researcher and educator Johnson O'Connor said that "a person's vocabulary level is the best single predictor of occupational success." Success in the workplace often depends upon communication skills.

Sabrina, fifteen, is strong linguistically. Her grandfather noticed her early ability to spell long words. Today, she speaks fluent French and Spanish and is *"keen to move onto other languages."* Her English teacher remarked on her *"excellent spoken vocabulary, expression and communication where she sees every class as an opportunity to improve"* and *"the study of English as a springboard to life."* Her mother agrees that her daughter is *"always up for new experiences"* and noted the emergence of original thinking in her creative writing.

Jude's teacher said it was clear that he benefited from exposure to a rich language environment: *"He is an excellent communicator"* with *"superb spoken vocabulary and usage. In 'Joseph and the Amazing Technicolor Dreamcoat' it was noticeable that he was around adults a lot."* Jude has a *"real flair for English."* His capacity for creative writing is evident: *"He is an ideas boy. During lockdown he wrote a play with his mates and came top in the English Challenge at school"*, says his father. Jude agreed: *"I love creative writing and making an image as detailed as possible."*

Lucy, eleven, is highly imaginative and exceptionally artistic. This comes through in a capacity for written language which her teacher described as 'amazing'. An amusing, unassuming child, she says, *"I'm good at coming up with my own ideas for things, even random things. If the teacher said to write a story, I'd come up with one, no problem."* At seven, her teacher differentiated her work to meet Lucy's thirst for language.

How to help – language usage

Strategies for parents and caregivers:

☞ Notice early talkers and their potential for advanced vocabulary and sentence structure. Gifted infants may become quite frustrated if they can't make the sounds they want. Teaching babies sign language may be a good way to help them express themselves.[54]

☞ Expose gifted children to the wide range of spoken text types, their purposes and potential audiences (e.g. stories, interviews, debates). They can provide endless learning opportunities and outlets.

☞ Use these spoken text types as a springboard to different writing styles – letter, narrative, descriptive, procedural (e.g. recipe), explanatory (e.g. manual), persuasive (e.g. advert). Show the child how each style is used for a specific purpose.

☞ Gifted learners love opportunities to play with language. Try tongue twisters, limericks, metaphors, puns and onomatopoeia. Use jokes, song lyrics and poems as you introduce vocabulary. As the interviews show, gifted learners can have an alert and subtle sense of humour.

Strategies for teachers and schools:

☞ Show the gifted learner examples of genres from fiction and non-fiction: fantasy, crime, horror, romance and so on. Discuss the various reasons for choosing a particular genre, who the audience would be, and what that style of writing looks like.

☞ Encourage the learner to compile their own writing portfolio with examples of written genres they have collected as well as samples of their own work in the different genres. Writing is an activity that allows students to differentiate at their own level, and it is a failsafe method of having work to engage and extend the gifted learner.

---

54 Thompson, R.H., Cotnoir-Bichelman, N.M., McKerchar, P.M., Tate, T.L. & Dancho, K.A. (2013) Enhancing Early Communication through Infant Sign Training. *Journal of Applied Behaviour Analysis* 40(1).

- Never let spelling hold back the emerging gifted writer. Encourage the gifted child to compile their own personal 'developmental dictionary' with the words they need. Provide them with word banks to scaffold their topic (this is particularly helpful for EAL (English as an Additional Language) students).

- Some gifted learners procrastinate and don't know how to get started. Sentence starters may help. Or help your gifted learners get started by setting writing goals (e.g. "today I will describe my main character"). This is another means of differentiation.

- Ensure that vocabulary instruction is an integral part of your language and literacy teaching. Include subject-specific vocabularies from maths, science and other subject areas. Develop a vocabulary wall and consider giving the gifted learner responsibility for it.

- Before asking students to commit a new word to memory, ensure that they understand its real meaning. Marilee Sprenger calls this 'recoding', and it is an opportunity to correct any misconceptions before the wrong meaning gets embedded in long-term memory.

- Use Content and Language Integrated Learning (CLIL). Sometimes referred to as bilingual education, this involves learners studying a subject such as science in a foreign language, thereby learning two things at once.[55]

---

[55] Sahin, C. (Celik), & Schmidt, O. (2014) Teaching English Activities for the Gifted and Talented Students. *Journal for the Education of Gifted Young Scientists* 1(53).

Chapter 11: Creativity and imaginative expression

Gifted children can be imaginative and abstract thinkers, but there are interesting differences between gifted learners and creative thinkers. Nurturing creativity in gifted children is vital for their development and happiness. It improves self-esteem, helps them understand and accept their talents, and provides permission and a vehicle for self-expression. Creatively gifted kids who are given an enriching environment within which to explore their skills can become more focused and goal oriented. This chapter focuses on gifted learners who also exhibit creativity.

> ### Key Point
> Nurturing creativity in gifted children is vital for their development and happiness.

Rayleen Clancy, a practising artist and art educator, said that real creativity is a "willingness to try, to explore new risky ideas and maybe fail, to spark off in a completely different way – not the beaten path".[56] The poet and playwright W.B. Yeats did that with 'automatic writing', as did James Joyce with *Ulysses*. Both continue to be recognised and celebrated worldwide today for their creative genius. Clancy continued: "Going into the dark, the unknown, the fear, is where you find genius". Frequently, she added, the real genius is someone who may be at first rejected because they're before their time and the proof of their genius is only recognised posthumously.

She instanced the case of the Swedish artist Hilma af Klint (1862-1944) a pioneering master of abstraction and automatic drawing who is only today recognised as hugely influential, more than seventy years after her death. As a result, art history has had to be rewritten. Listening to the US trailer for the recent documentary on af Klint's life, *Beyond the Visible*, one commentator said of her original thinking: "She had a mind of her own and painted like nobody else". Another said: "She walked away at the same time as she made the way; it's not easy to be a pioneer."[57]

It's important to note that creative giftedness is somewhat 'bittersweet', in that as well as being a gift it can also be a burden, a responsibility that can weigh heavily on young shoulders. The interviews show that gifted learners who are creative are frequently misunderstood. They struggle with their giftedness; sometimes nothing is good enough, and they can

---

56 Clancy, R. (2021) Cill Rialaig Arts Centre
57 ZeitgeistFilms (2020) *Beyond the Visible: Hilma af Klint* – official US trailer [online].

suffer as a result. For this reason, it is important that they are identified, 'seen' for who and what they are and supported in the process by parents, caregivers and educators.

Recognising the creatively gifted child

Tali Shenfield makes the point that not all intellectually gifted learners excel academically.[58] I agree, and that is why this book recognises the existence of giftedness in a single domain or more. Hence, differentiating intellectually gifted children from creatively gifted children is challenging. Parents and educators can't simply look at a child's grades or examine which subjects they excel in and determine whether they are intellectually or creatively gifted. A useful comparison tool is provided by Kingore in Appendix 4. It outlines essential differences between a high achiever, a gifted learner and a creative thinker.

Moreover, not all creative individuals demonstrate remarkable skill in the visual or performing arts. Some creatively gifted children show a more philosophical bent (see **Nina**'s case below), rather than taking an obvious interest in drawing, creative writing, music or acting. Hence, to identify creative giftedness, parents and educators need to examine a child's core traits. They must consider the ways in which their child thinks, not just where they prefer to direct their energy. This is an important message.

While every child is unique, several traits are common to a majority of creatively gifted children and can therefore serve as useful indicators.

Openness

Creatively gifted children live in a world of endless possibilities. Where an intellectually gifted child will debate the correct answer, a creatively gifted child will think of multiple potential answers or hypothetical scenarios. They enjoy experimenting with thought and finding exceptions to rules. "**Dylan** can go off on a tangent in class and has to express himself", says his mother. "He might lose the audience in the process and not care, his need for space to express himself is so immediate." Unsurprisingly, this manner of thinking and expression can lead to misunderstandings and friction.

---

58 Shenfield T. (2021) What is Creative Giftedness, and How Can Creativity be Nurtured in Gifted Children? *Advanced Psychology* [online].

Inventiveness

Creatively gifted children can be original thinkers, seeking new and unusual combinations among items of information.[59] They are excellent at connecting seemingly disparate concepts in order to generate fresh ideas.

Rhys ably demonstrates this with his interest in technology and innovation, improving an existing product to create something new. Creatively gifted children see problems and situations from striking and unexpected angles. This can also be the case with dyslexic children or adults – at times, too, their opinions may seem bizarre or contradictory to outside observers.

Lucy, who had extreme sensory issues as a baby and young child, demonstrates remarkable skill in the visual arts. She is also inventive in her thinking and sees subtle relationships between thoughts: *"I can see how things relate to each other, for example a Teletubbies character and Yoda in Star Wars. When I'm bored, I start to think 'why does this remind me of this?', so I created the two pictures side by side to prove my point."*

Distractibility

Because creatively gifted children are constantly overflowing with ideas, they can have trouble staying on task – even when engaged in voluntary activities. These young people tend to start a lot of projects but struggle to complete the great majority of them. They can be preoccupied with imaginative fantasy, rather than internalising information, and they can daydream a great deal. (Note: it is important to rule out ADHD before attributing traits of distractibility to creative giftedness.)

Dylan is easily distracted and sometimes won't see tasks through to completion. For example, when doing homework or music practice the smallest thing will distract him and he will stop. Dylan admits to having trouble focusing yet, when he worked with me on a one-off project, he showed he was open to new ideas to help him *"knuckle down."*

Intuition

Creatively gifted children rely heavily on intuition. They often feel like they 'just know' the correct way to solve a problem, without being sure how they arrived at their conclusions. Dylan's mother, an opera singer, stresses that this is *"the norm"* for creative people; they start something and may have no idea where it will end up, relying on their intuition to guide them.

---

[59] Whitmore, J.R. (1985) *Characteristics of Intellectually Gifted Children.* 1985 Digest, Revised. ERIC Clearinghouse on Handicapped and Gifted Children, 1920 Association.

They also have a great capacity for empathy. **Olga**'s mother remarked that of her three daughters, Olga had empathy in abundance and was able to determine what other people were feeling. Her teacher saw her carry this into her music, and said Olga was *"among the most talented"* she had ever seen. Her violin playing at age nine or ten was *"haunting"*, it was played with such feeling. She believed that Olga could be a professional musician.

Visual artists like **Lucy** project themselves onto the canvas when they paint: *"I love art and am naturally good at it. I have to really concentrate with the sketching, making it really pretty. My class entered an art competition last week and it took me four-and-a-half hours to do my picture on an A3 sheet. My teacher had to allow me to finish it off at home."*

Similarly, **Jude** demonstrates a great depth of empathy for the characters he performs, already winning four key roles as a child actor in West End shows. *"Jude is highly respected in the acting world; when he performed in assembly, he had twenty-one-thousand views within twenty-four hours"*, says his teacher. Highly intuitive, and loving improvisation and 'personification', Jude is aware that *"the audience wants to see the child, not what the adult thinks the child should be."*

Individualism

Though many gifted children may have a tendency to come across as being somewhat eccentric, creatively gifted kids are often radically different. They usually show a marked lack of interest in 'fitting in', preferring to pursue their own unique style of expression. This can make it difficult for them to participate in group learning. As adolescents, these individuals are often drawn to niche subcultures and unconventional modes of living.

Today, **Luka** is a twenty-four-year-old gay man who also performs in drag. Reflecting on school, Luka says he coped with the peer group by *"learning to adapt and not flaunt my knowledge"*. It was a leveller for him: *"I was less concerned about being the best or showing off what I knew, although I still did well enough in tests. I figured out I was funny and used that to get by."* Giftedness wasn't always easy to bear: *"I think about things differently; if I was more logical than creative maybe it would be easier for me."*

Skill in the performing arts

Luka's creativity was his stand-out gift. At the age of ten *"he played the three stages of Scrooge in the school play,"* recalls his mother, *"and that was the first time I saw him singing and performing."* Later Luka recalls that he *"arranged a medley of four pop songs and won the school talent competition."* His music teacher also recognised his gift: *"The minute Luka touched a keyboard I knew he understood music as a language. You cannot make a child musical. A person that can hold you by the way they play, that's Luka; he just has it naturally."* Luka has demonstrated his creative talent many times in public, in shows and events. Today, he works as a content analyst completely through French, demonstrating the link between music and language: *"language, accents and music all connect in my head."*

Gifted musically, **Ruby** could whistle by the age of two and is described by her mother as *"in the zone"* musically. She was nurtured early by her parents and teachers; her father said: *"Showing an interest is most important, and be on the lookout for their special talents."* Ruby, now twenty-four and a psychology graduate, has an exceptional singing voice and performs regularly in public. *"The voice is her instrument,"* says her mother. *"She can create the harmony as the melody is being played for the first time."*

The philosophical child

Nina is strongly motivated by social justice. She says her *"main gift is history; I've loved history books since I was eight, for example on the Battle of Britain, the Greeks and the two World Wars."* Arguing that teachers don't do enough history in school, she is a *"human rights advocate"* who reads *"loads of books about feminists."* Her teacher described her as a *"complex little character"* but well able to *"hold her space"*. She dressed up as a suffragette at Halloween but was disappointed that others didn't understand. School is not always easy for Nina. Reflecting on her peers, she says: *"They don't see me really - they ignore me and just think of themselves. At school I feel different to everyone and feel that I'm the odd one out."* She can grow quite frustrated at times: *"I just wish every child would shut up, listen and learn!".*

How to help – nurturing creativity

Strategies for parents and caregivers:

☞ Allow gifted learners to be themselves, which may be very different from others, and observe and encourage them. Be on the lookout for talents that may not always be cultivated at school, and that may benefit from extra tuition outside the classroom environment.

☞ Give them the means to express themselves. Provide access to art supplies, a cheap camera, clothes for dress-up and toys that facilitate creative play. Notice what they are drawn to and get lost in; Let them make a mess and leave partly completed projects out for another day.

☞ While your child is small, teach them to 'play pretend'.⁶⁰ If they love dinosaurs, suggest that you both pretend to be prehistoric creatures. Imaginative play has been shown to improve skills that are essential for creativity, and in the right environment children do this naturally.

☞ Include free time in the timetable. While gifted learners benefit from routine, the mind also needs unstructured time to generate new ideas. Make sure they aren't perpetually occupied with homework and extra-curricular activities, and give them space to pursue their own interests.

Strategies for teachers and schools:

☞ Help gifted learners to explore and take risks with their ideas. Debate concepts and challenge their views, but never shut down their ideas. The gifted learner needs to understand that it's okay to disagree, and that doing so won't make them wrong or foolish. This is important.

☞ Help creatively gifted children to be metacognitive, to consider the thinking behind their thinking, by raising their awareness of creative traits such as distractibility and individualism so they recognise them in themselves. This way they can learn to check in with themselves and become better able to self-manage.

☞ Expose creatively gifted learners to outside influences by bringing in artists, performers and drama groups to inspire students. Provide outlets for learners to show, challenge and validate their talents by putting on assemblies, concerts, exhibitions and competitions.

☞ Research has shown that multiple aspects of a classroom environment (e.g. deadlines, surveillance, external rewards) can lessen the intrinsic motivation that feeds creativity.⁶¹ Keep this in mind – let gifted learners be themselves, observe and encourage them, but don't ignore them.

---

60 Shenfield, T. (2016) How to Engage in Play With Your Children – and Enjoy It. *Advanced Psychology* [online].

61 Amabile, T.M. (1983) The social psychology of creativity: A componential conceptualization. *Journal of Personality and Social Psychology* 45(2) 357-376.

Chapter 12: Sense of humour

Gifted learners have a great facility to manipulate language for their own purposes. Have you ever wondered who makes up all the jokes we hear? The classics, the riddles, the knock-knock jokes? Those jokes were more than likely made up by some very smart people who possess an uncommon wit and grasp of language – in essence, gifted comedians. Research has shown that gifted children have a notably good sense of humour, with higher mean scores for spontaneous mirth response and comprehension on the pun and satire items.[62] They show an unusual imagination and a heightened sense of humour borne out of a deep sense of curiosity that is there from the beginning of their lives.[63] Some describe it as 'zany'.[64]

> **Key Point**
>
> *Gifted learners show a heightened sense of humour borne out of a deep sense of curiosity that is there from the beginning of their lives.*

Our gifted learners were often interested in jokes and humour. Teenager **Amy** is *"very original, not interested in copying, would lose and find you with words and loves solving riddles"*, says her mother. Paediatrician **Miguel** describes his sense of humour as *"nuanced"* and his teacher agrees: *"It was clear he got it in a subtle way, even at age six"*. At seven, **Nina** understands *"timing when it's okay to speak and okay to joke."* Taken together, the learners also make it clear that a sense of humour is a key requirement for parents and teachers – they will test you! At the same time, humour can be a very useful device for putting things into perspective, avoiding the trap of becoming locked into worry, and not taking oneself too seriously.

Adult sense of humour

Gifted students love relating to adults and can have a more adult sense of humour than their peers, revealing a more sophisticated sense of what is funny. While a classmate might find humour in a 'poop joke', a gifted learner might be greatly amused by a pun or a Shakespeare joke that other children do not understand. Sarcasm is another good indicator of being gifted, as it is very abstract and most young children

---

62 Shade, R. (1991) Verbal Humor in Gifted Students and Students in the General Population: A Comparison of Spontaneous Mirth and Comprehension. *Journal for the Education of the Gifted*. 14(2).
63 Caldwell, J. (1998) How to identify and nurture our gifted children'. *Independent*.ie [online].
64 Gross, G. (2013) Who Is the Gifted Child? *HuffPost Life* [online].

think in a concrete manner.⁶⁵ **Olga** was, according to her mother, *"quick-witted with the ability to laugh at herself, for example playing games of 'Frustration' at three."* Her primary teacher noted that she had a *"smart, cynical sense of humour"* in class.

Gifted learners often find an ally that they relate to humorously within the family. **Emma**'s mother said: *"She and her father are in tune; they have a wicked sense of humour."* **Ava**'s mother describes her as *"very funny; she keeps the family going with her humour. She and her Dad are like this."*

Humour preferences

A study by Doris Bergen on humour preferences among seventy-four gifted children aged seven to twelve produced results that are echoed in the case study interviews.⁶⁶ The study explored sense of humour, comprehension of riddles, learners' humorous media preferences, explanations of funniness, and the ability to produce, understand and figure out riddle 'punch-lines'. Bergen's gifted children rated themselves high on sense of humour, with most media humour exhibiting "conceptual word play with multiple meanings". She noted that girls differed from boys in being more likely to take on the 'spectator role' – noticing and laughing at funny situations.

The majority of gifted learners interviewed for this book are rated as having an 'alert and subtle sense of humour' by either a parent or teacher – although not necessarily by themselves, which is interesting. I suspect that they regarded it as their normal way of being. For example, **Rhys**, fifteen, is *"very creative; he delivers killer one-liners, summarising a situation very quickly"*, says his mother. Likewise, **Dylan**, twelve, has, as his mother says, a *"taste for the double entendre and is exceptional at mimicking people. That can be extremely funny – the Trump impressions, the off-the cuff content which can be very quick witted. So, in the moment it can be quite funny."*

Most children produced a correctly told joke or riddle and gave accurate explanations of funniness. **Sasha**'s father described his daughter as having a *"good sense of humour – no dull moments, there's always a joke."* Ava demonstrated *"smart humour"* – she *"got it"* and *"would always get involved in the fun but wouldn't just laugh at anything"*, said her teacher.

---

65 Stanley, T. (2017) *How to spot a gifted child.* edCircuit [online].
66 Bergen, D. (2009) Gifted children's humor preferences, sense of humor, and Comprehension of riddles. Humor: *International Journal of Humor Research* 22(4) 419-436.

Disposition and sense of humour

There is no doubt that gifted learners are a diverse group when it comes to their disposition. Some are worriers and carry the world on their shoulders, whereas others are more light-hearted. **Ethan**, now twenty-three, *"laughed his way through primary school"*, says his teacher. **Melissa**, now fifty-eight, held court with her circle and had a good sense of humour to keep friends so close and loyal to her in secondary school. *"One day she asked me a question in maths,"* her teacher recalls, *"pointing out her approach in her copy. As I was absorbing it, I noticed her face was turned towards me in curiosity, watching with amusement while I sorted it out!"*

> **Key Point**
>
> Gifted learners are diverse when it comes to disposition. Some carry the world on their shoulders, whereas others wear their giftedness lightly.

When **Lucy** was seven, her teacher said that her *"sense of humour comes out in small groups."* Naturally amusing, in an off-the-cuff manner, Lucy has a resilient ability to not take herself too seriously: *"The boys call me Alexa sometimes because I'm the smartest in my class, but in a friendly way not a mean way"* or *"when adults zone out, I just have to tell them again."* **Sasha**, though very committed to her studies, believes in *"not taking things that seriously."* Her tutor commented: *"Teaching Sasha at 7.30am on Saturday mornings provided a little entertainment. She arrived one day before I'd got up, so I met her at the door after a little wait, saying 'You were here before I thought of getting up!' She just laughed."*

On the other hand **Jess**, now twenty-nine, took herself very seriously as a child and teenager and wasn't interested in experimenting with creative areas at all. He teacher neatly captures something she once said: *"I'm not doing anything with glitter!"* So focused was she on getting into Harvard University that anything that didn't appear to immediately support that end was dismissed. There was no room for a sense of humour, and she says it was only after her dream wasn't realised that she became more *"flexible"* and started to develop herself holistically and work on her own happiness.

Others like **Ruby**, now twenty-four, find that humour can help when they are uncertain or lacking in confidence. Joking and gentle pushing from the boys in her band helps her to cope with her *"toxic perfectionism"*, enabling her to give new songs or pieces a go. Similarly, Nina's teacher carefully uses jokes and light-hearted humour to help Nina come out of herself when she's feeling down. Humour turns her thinking around and helps her feel better.

How to help – sense of humour

Strategies for parents and caregivers:

☞ Gifted learners can be naturally sarcastic and cynical, without meaning to cause hurt. Discuss how their words can impact others, and the appropriateness of sarcasm in a given context, reminding them that it is often used to mock and/or to convey contempt.

☞ An innovative ability with words is a hallmark of the verbally gifted child. Expose them to age-appropriate riddles, jokes, satire, puns and multiple meanings of words across contexts and cultures.

☞ Help the gifted learner to see different points of view. Try a stuffed giraffe toy to show how, with his long neck, he can see things from a different perspective than, for example, a hasty, snapping crocodile.

☞ Gifted learners may struggle to navigate society's rules and see that it is sometimes best to hold one's tongue. Discuss when it is and is not appropriate to tell a joke, offer positive criticism or correct someone.

Strategies for teachers and schools:

☞ Draw the gifted learner's attention to their facility with language and remind them how useful jokes, funny stories and images can be when recalling content. They may already do this unconsciously, but not realise that it is a valid and memorable study strategy.

☞ Ask them to identify examples of sarcasm, cynicism or irony in an author's work, for class sharing. Encourage them to identify ways in which they could use these literary devices in their own writing.

☞ Joke creation should not be dismissed – it merges the intellectual and creative, and it is a skill we should give learners the chance to try out in the classroom. Ground rules are important, of course.

☞ Choose a 'zany' TV advert or jingle for discussion. Discuss its images, messages and taglines. Ask gifted learners to create their own advert for a given audience – you'll quickly find out who the potential marketeers are!

Part 4: Motivation and leadership

Chapter 13: Motivation and task commitment

Motivation may be defined as "the process whereby goal-directed activity is instigated and sustained."[67] It is fascinating to study the motivation levels of gifted learners. From talking to gifted learners across the age ranges, it would appear that their motivation and dedication generally follows their desire and intent at a personal level. Beyond this, it is influenced by wider factors including expectancy value, intrinsic and extrinsic motivation, goal orientations, self-efficacy/self-perception, and attribution theory.[68]

> **Key Point**
>
> Motivation and dedication generally follows the gifted learner's desire and intent at a personal level.

We often equate motivation exclusively with school achievement. However, it's important to note that some children may be highly motivated to achieve goals that are unrelated to school. A gifted teenager, for example, may be interested in creating a volunteer community group to help children with special needs.

Generally, gifted learners can be very highly motivated. Speaking with a teacher of a gifted programme about her experience with gifted children, she says "They'll stick with it even if they don't get it right first time, they are what Renzulli calls task-committed." This is certainly evident in many of the learners interviewed for this book. This is not to suggest that their motivation is a constant – it can wane when appropriate learning challenges and opportunities are not in place (see Chapter 14). Neither does it suggest that all gifted learners achieve at their level. Learning difficulties in gifted children can sometimes lead to under-achievement, and these twice exceptional (2e) learners require careful attention.[69]

---

67 Kadioglu, C. & Uzuntiryaki, E. (2008) *Motivational Factors Contributing to Turkish High School Students' Achievement in Gases and Chemical Reactions*. ERIC [online].

68 Clinkenbeard, P.R. (2012) Motivation and gifted students: implications of theory and research. *Psychology in the Schools* 49 (7).

69 Bainbridge, C. (2020) *How to Motivate Your Gifted Child*. Verywell Family [online].

Intrinsic motivation and being goal-driven

Many gifted learners are highly motivated and task-committed, often demonstrating a strong awareness that school and education is linked to life purpose. **Ethan**'s motivation came entirely from himself: "*It was clear he was enjoying learning; he was fast-paced and would light up at the notion of a new topic*", said his primary teacher. Now a medical student, Ethan says he "*always associated academic success with life success*" and is willing to undertake "*eleven years of stressful exams*" to be a cardiologist.

Jude's level of motivation as a child actor is outstanding. Without it he wouldn't be able to achieve all he does – to manage an exacting schedule in a private school and star in West End shows simultaneously, sometimes having to leave school as early as midday. He is mature compared with his peers, and because his desire to succeed in his roles is so strong, he takes full responsibility for his schoolwork. If he misses a lesson due to his theatre commitments, he will make it up. "*He is ahead of the game and takes outstanding responsibility for his learning*", says his teacher.

Sabrina displays good levels of intrinsic motivation: "*I am an independent learner, more than happy to do it by myself.*" Her mother and teacher agree that motivation is a strong point: "*She is serious about school and aware that school is linked to life purpose*", says her mother. Her teacher adds that she is "*really focused*". Sabrina displays the 'outstanding responsibility and independence in classroom work" indicated in the GFL.

Miguel was "*always motivated in a steady way, it came from himself*", says his teacher, while his mother says that: "*His interest in medicine came from when he was very small and he got on really well with the GP, and, ironically, he spent time in hospital when he was very young.*" **Sasha** is intrinsically motivated and goal oriented. "*She would arrive for early morning private tuition in maths when most teenagers would want to sleep*", said her teacher. Her father commented, "*We don't know where we got her, she is that different from the others.*"

While much can go well in terms of school achievement for gifted learners, career paths for high achievers can sometimes prove problematic without the right support, advice and direction. This was the case with **Jess**: "*I was more invested in achieving the A than how it translated into life.*" Her mother agreed that Jess "*drove herself at an unsustainable level in secondary school.*" On reflection, she regrets that both Jess and her parents didn't have better career guidance available for Jess's sake.

Resourcefulness

Gifted learners can also demonstrate extraordinary levels of resourcefulness. At fifteen, **Ava** is *"highly motivated"* and *"very resourceful"*, says her mother. Her teacher said she was always keen: *"there was no such thing as 'do I have to?' with Ava, she always wanted to."* At just eleven, **Lucy** is resourceful too. Her concentration and dedication flow from her desire to produce great artwork: *"You have to concentrate with the sketching, to make it really pretty."*

Jess was a very headstrong and independent child: *"My way was always right."* She was focused and even as a little girl *"she wanted her easel on vacation so she could have her plans; she was relieved to learn she could plan on paper!"* Her teacher in the gifted programme said motivation was Jess's number one gift: *"She would ask if she could do extra stuff, always academically advanced and task-committed."* **Greg**, forty-two, was, according to his teacher, *"motivated to overcome any challenge as a teenager. Once it mattered to him the motivation came from himself."*

Jude has a strong focus on the exam system and a top university, saying *"I don't have a fixed mindset, I see a challenge as a mountain to be climbed, I'm up for it."* It seems he is putting the whole picture together for himself: *"I used to be ninety percent on task, now I wish I worked harder."* Recognising the huge commitment involved from this young boy, I asked Jude's teacher, also the Vice-Principal, if he thought Jude could sustain it: *"I think he can because of his grounded approach. With the dedication and support of his family, I don't see him pushed too far."* Jude is a good example of where the personal and environmental factors of motivation come to bear.

How to help – using the TARGET model to engage learners

TARGET is a model for structuring classroom practices in a way that promotes student motivation.[70] It is very interesting and can be usefully adapted to suit the needs of gifted learners. The following is a brief guide.

 Task: To motivate gifted learners, provide a variety of student tasks of optimal difficulty and challenge including new content. Develop their higher-order thinking skills by starting with analysis, evaluation and creative synthesis (Bloom's taxonomy), and allow them to pick up basic comprehension and application of the material as they go.

---

70 Cecchini, J., Fernandez-Rio, J., Méndez-Giménez, A., Cecchini, C. & Martins, L. (2014) Epstein's TARGET Framework and Motivational Climate in Sport: Effects of a Field-Based, Long-Term Intervention Program. *International Journal of Sports Science & Coaching* 9(6): 1325-1340.

Autonomy: Give them autonomy by engaging them in shared decision-making and providing a choice of tasks and materials to work on. A menu approach is a good idea. Encourage them to talk about their choice so they experience the feeling of autonomy.

 Recognition: Rewards or extrinsic motivation work to a point with some gifted learners, but they can be detrimental and should not be relied upon. Better to nurture intrinsic motivation as well. Providing individual feedback where you compare their work to a standard or against their own starting point is more beneficial than comparing them to others. Recognition should be aimed at learning and improvement, not performing best on work that is too easy.

 Grouping: See a class as a community of learners. Provide students with opportunities to be involved in flexible grouping arrangements within the class – mixed ability, same ability and mixed gender – and see what works best. Remember, you are also teaching them how to negotiate and survive in some testing social situations!

 Evaluation: Grading and evaluation should be for the purpose of assessing effort and improvement if the goal is to increase mastery motivation. High-achieving students can be challenged to improve and master new material at a higher expectancy level. The reason for this may need to be explained to them.

 Time: Adjust the amount of time and workload allocated so that students can experience maximum success and mastery. Ensure that there are further options (not just more of the same) available for 'early finishers', for example learning centres, independent reading time or small research projects of their own choosing.

Validation and feedback

Parents and teachers who provide feedback and connect with the gifted learner at their level are tailoring the intervention to suit them. This is excellent practice. All gifted learners benefit from linked feedback, and some need it more than others. **Sabrina** loves external validation and feedback: *"I like when my work is rewarded, a reason to do better, work harder, it's validated, for example when my essay is shown to the class."* This may suggest that she doubts herself at times, which is a very human response. On the other hand, **Miguel** didn't seem to need external validation, although he received it: *"He was praised for his results, even with a summer job, but he knew he wasn't doing it for his parents, he was doing it for himself"*, says his mother.

Work ethic

Another striking factor of many gifted learners is a strong work ethic. **Ethan**, a high-achieving medical student, will do whatever it takes to achieve his goal. So intent is he on being a doctor, and ultimately a cardiologist, that he says: *"there is nothing I like more than a day when I can spend twelve hours in the library."* **Miguel** is further on in his career journey and a successful practising paediatrician. *"He always had a strong work ethic, it is a feature of his life"*, says his mother.

Jude's father said that his son *"has a real work ethic and phenomenal energy. He was only ten when he starred in his demanding role in 'Caroline, or Change'."* Jude's desire to perform in shows is so great that he's prepared to put in the extra commitment required. He and his father share a common language and understanding about his future: *"Jude has a real ability to work hard; he is a growth mindset kind of guy."* Strong family support and communication are not to be under-estimated. Jude's father keeps him grounded, and there is a shared understanding that if his schoolwork slips then Jude will have to forego the shows. External motivation, you may say, but his internal desire and motivation to perform matches it.

How to help – motivation

Strategies for parents and caregivers:[76]

☞ Gifted children who can pursue their interests are more likely to keep their love of learning alive, so provide opportunities for your child to learn and explore. Help them make connections between their interests and schoolwork, which may not be immediately apparent.

☞ Gifted children love challenges, so turn homework into a game to motivate them to complete it and help avoid procrastination. Ask them to see how quickly they can get it done without mistakes.

☞ Sometimes learners lack motivation because they haven't yet been exposed to what may be a life passion. Don't rely on the school and keep an open mind – finding and pursuing interests is important.

☞ Teach your gifted learner early how to plan and manage their time effectively, and ensure they take regular breaks. Getting 'in the zone' is a fabulous feeling, but remind them to look after themselves too.

☞ Ensure that you invest in career guidance for your teen gifted learner to explore their interests and desire. There is a plethora of careers available that may suit them, of which they may be unaware.

Strategies for teachers and schools:[76]

☞ Help gifted learners to make connections between schoolwork and potential career areas. Notice the subjects and topics that really get them interested, for example the topic of climate change in geography. Explore world issues and problems that they may wish to help solve.

☞ Discuss desires and intentions, especially with learners who are not yet aware of them. Give them opportunities to hear themselves say what they want and allow room for them to change their mind.

☞ Sometimes children get overwhelmed by large tasks – not due to difficulty, but because they can't see the end in sight. Help them to see the large task as a series of smaller tasks or goals, and affirm them when they have achieved each sub-goal.

☞ Praise their efforts to succeed and make that praise specific. For example, instead of saying "good work", it's better to say something like "you really worked hard on your history project."

Chapter 14: Boredom

Are you a parent wondering why your nine-year-old son is still studying words from the class spelling list when they can already read at a secondary level standard? Or why your five-year-old daughter is still working on simple single-number addition when she mastered two-digits with regrouping a month ago? Life in a typical classroom, some might say. No one promised fun and games all the time, yet the amount of time gifted learners spend waiting, unchallenged, doing repetitive work, daydreaming and battling boredom can be greater than for other students in mainstream classes. So the question is, how do we manage the gifted learner in the mainstream classroom and accommodate their needs, along with those of perhaps thirty other students?

> ## Expert View
>
> *"Bored, for a gifted child, is better described as frustration. Repetition is a part of learning, but gifted children need far less repetition than most."*[78]
>
> Carolyn Kottmeyer

Eleven-year-old **Lucy** says that she is unchallenged with maths: *"I'm quite good at maths; I'd be sitting there not learning anything new for twenty minutes."* Somewhere at the back of their minds, all gifted learners know the joy of learning, the sense of innate curiosity, the spark of discovery when learning is not slow or tedious. But that experience may seem far removed from everyday life in mixed-ability classrooms that are tailored to the needs of the average or at-risk student only.

All the teachers interviewed acknowledged this challenge, bemoaning the fact that more accommodation for gifted learners wasn't part of their teacher-education formation and that more specialist programming was not available. **Olga**'s teacher said, *"My challenge was how to challenge her and cope with boredom. I really believe in the gifted learner's niche abilities."* To address this issue she upskilled in 'instructional leadership' and became a facilitator of teamwork: *"I saw my role as a conduit, a scaffold, providing the material and task, not necessarily knowing where it would go."*

With all that said, let's not panic. Boredom can be an opportunity for everyone to learn – teacher, parent and student. Each has a responsibility in the process. Good can come out of embracing it, accepting it, and learning how to deal with it effectively. It should be noted that many of the gifted learners interviewed did not complain about boredom at

---

71 Kottmeyer, C. (2020). *Never Say Bored!* Hoagies Gifted Education Page [online].

all – they were happy in their skin and managed to occupy themselves productively. This wasn't all down to their teachers, either – personality type played a key role. Olga's mother admits that her daughter "*was placid; if she was a difficult kid she could have disengaged.*" It should also be noted that, when children say they are bored in school, it is sometimes a 'catch-all' phrase where they may be communicating a need in a specific subject area.

What is boredom?

Boredom is a state of failing to find meaning. It is a deeply uncomfortable feeling; an emotional state that we all experience at some point. There's a distinction to be made between 'state' and 'trait': state boredom refers to feeling bored in a specific situation, while trait boredom refers to how susceptible one is to boredom generally. Trait boredom is correlated with self-control, anxiety, depression and substance use, and would not necessarily be within the remit of a teacher.[72] With regard to gifted learners, the problem arises when boredom becomes a stagnant source of negativity that kills a child's interest in learning. When that boredom is the result of poor curricular decisions, it is a signal for change and needs to be addressed.

Signs of boredom

While some gifted learners will express frustration directly to the teachers when bored, most complain at home. Parents can witness tears, outbursts and refusals to complete work they rate as 'stupid' and not worth their time. **Dylan**'s mother admits that her son has "*no patience with time-wasting, repetitive tasks.*" Having suppressed frustration all day at school, bored gifted learners can batter their family with misdirected anger. Parents must weather their child's disappointment, limit conflict at home, empathise with their child's experience, and take care not to fuel further frustration by showing too much of their own distress. Dylan's mother accepted that, along with the teacher, she had a part to play in addressing the problem.

Gifted learners' frustration will generally emerge in one of two ways:

- **Acting out:** Some children entertain themselves by talking too much, becoming the class clown, or causing trouble. **Luka** said he realised "*he could be funny.*" Boredom became an issue for him in upper primary and secondary school. According to his mother, he was very

---

[72] Psychology Today (2022) Boredom. *Psychology Today* [online].

"*impatient*" and "*easily bored.*" This presented challenges: "*I would finish early and be left there to my own devices. Not being challenged lead me to act out.*" For other learners, frustration may be expressed through aggression – bullying, fighting, using their verbal skills to manipulate other classmates. It is complex. Parents then receive feedback from teachers about their child's behaviours.

- **Internalising:** These children don't show outward signs of distress, but instead become shy, withdrawn, or develop physical symptoms such as stomach aches or headaches. They may become anxious, have difficulty getting up in the morning, or refuse to go to school, citing physical complaints or vague fears. Often, they fall below the radar, and teachers may not recognize their distress. **Nina**'s mother gave up her job as a social worker when Nina was six so that she could be home each day to help Nina debrief after school. In the interview I said to her mother: "*Nina comes across as quite happy to me*", to which she responded, "*That's because I spend up to an hour and a half listening to her after school each day.*" Nina agreed.

Whether the child's boredom is expressed overtly or indirectly, it can create lasting damage. Boredom fuels apathy, disregard for authority, underachievement and sometimes a complete loss of interest in school. Even those gifted children who are remarkably patient and tolerate the situation can be left with a distorted perception of their abilities. They may assume all academic challenges will be easy, never learn to struggle or push themselves, and fear failure. **Maria**, a forty-two-year-old engineer who suspects she may be on the autism spectrum, was regularly left unchallenged at school and feels she "*never realised her true potential.*"

 How to help – managing boredom

Strategies for parents and caregivers:

 If schools appear unable to challenge gifted learners, parents need to ask for help. Start by respectfully asking the teacher's advice. Teachers are often unaware of how a child is behaving at home until they are told. Initiating a conversation and building a positive relationship is key.

 There may be resources available outside school such as specialist centres for gifted and talented youth. Ask the teacher what he or she would suggest, and how you can work together to improve things.

☞ Parents can also ask the teacher for alternative activities for their child when classwork is completed, or provide material from home. Make sure your child always has a book with them in physical or digital form.

☞ If the boredom is mostly at home, look at the home environment. Is the timing of homework suitable – is your child hungry, or missing a favourite TV show? These factors will impact mood and motivation.

☞ Be patient, tactful and persistent. All children deserve an education that meets their needs. For some, this may mean a new school or home schooling. Parents must act in the best interest of their child.

Strategies for teachers and schools:

☞ Don't panic if you hear the words "I'm bored." The best response may simply be: "Me too – what shall we do about it?" As a teacher, I knew if I was bored with my teaching approach that it was time for change.

☞ Provide a mental escape route for when learners finish work early. For example, encourage them to create more in-depth questions, research an uplifting individual, write a poem or compose a tune. Having a diary for their own reflections is a great habit to cultivate.

☞ Encourage the child to explore why they feel bored. If they realise an activity isn't valuable for them, let them come up with suggestions as to how to engage in more worthwhile activities in future.

☞ Engage learners in teamwork where everyone has an opportunity to bring something to the table. Explore teams with mixed and high ability. Draw on resources such as 'Stretch, Bend and Boggle'.[73]

☞ Collaborate with learners and their parents to create a plan of action similar to an Individual Education Plan for gifted learners, especially those who are unfulfilled. Monitor progress and check in regularly.

---

[73] Stokes, B. (2004) *Stretch, Bend and Boggle: A week-by-week maths program for developing logic and problem-solving skills*. Hawker Brownlow Education.

The benefits of boredom

Boredom is not all bad. As a motivator towards change, it can lead to new ideas, reflection and creativity. It can propel new routes of play and self-entertainment, help to develop self-reliance and relationship skills, and fuel the search for novelty, including setting new goals or embarking on new adventures.[74] Boredom can provide "unexpected opportunities for children to learn and grow".[75] When children are left to amuse themselves (without screens!) they develop new ways to keep busy. They learn to tolerate uncertainty, exercise creativity, communicate with others and negotiate conflict, all invaluable life lessons that are critical to the world we live in.

We must dispel the myth that children need to be occupied every minute of their day. This is not healthy for the mind. In short, we can do our gifted learners a favour by letting them figure out how to occupy and entertain themselves. In addition to accommodating their individual needs in the classroom, this is where I believe we need to focus. Set out below are some ideas for approaching boredom in a more positive way, and for moving toward a mindset that embraces its potential benefits in all areas of life. Eastern cultures have long understood the value of this, believing it to be a path to enlightenment and a higher level of consciousness.

How to help – embracing boredom

☞ The study of boredom isn't boring! Reframe boredom by playing a game of 'let's be bored' and seeing what happens. If it's boring for two minutes, do it for four. If it's still boring, do it for eight. Sooner or later the child will realise it's not boring at all, and they have control.

☞ Show the child how to become a journalist or scientist by studying their environment. What can they see and hear? By bringing their analytical powers to bear, they can make almost anything interesting.

☞ Prepare worksheets with pictures of wildflowers or trees that grow in the immediate surroundings. The task is to find them, note their location and discover more about them. This activates the child's powers of focus, concentration, observation and memory.

---

74 Heshmat, S. (2020) 5 Benefits of Boredom. *Psychology Today* [online].
75 Escalante, A. (2018) Boredomtunity: Why Boredom Is the Best Thing for Our Kids. *Psychology Today*. [online].

Meditation can mitigate boredom, and it can be practised in all sorts of situations – for example, while waiting for a class. Ask the child to try using this time to reflect on an aspect of life for which they feel grateful.

 Explore gratitude further. Ask the child where their mind takes them when they consider people, events or places that inspire feelings of gratitude. Encourage them to document this in a journal. As well as occupying themselves, they will boost their intrapersonal intelligence.

Chapter 15: Competitiveness

The relationship between competition, motivation and giftedness is an intriguing one. Some gifted learners are motivated by competition with themselves, to improve a personal best, while others can be motivated by competition with others – they are in it to win. This chapter explores how gifted learners view competition, the differences between boys and girls, and the benefits and potential pitfalls of competition for the gifted.

> **Key Point**
>
> Some gifted learners are motivated by competition with themselves, while others can be motivated by competition with others – they are in it to win.

Competition orientation matters

Writers in the field of gifted education promote competition. But the competitive style of the gifted learner matters. The key is how individuals orient themselves towards the competition – essentially, are the students fuelled by the desire to improve their performance, or is it a drive to one-up someone else?[76] The interviews bear this out. Some gifted learners were clearly in it to compete and win, whereas others were more measured and interested in achieving their personal best. Competition is healthier when students are competing against their own standards or previous records, or collaborating in a team, than when they are simply trying to beat others.

Research has also revealed that gifted students are task-oriented.[77] Task-orientation was found to be related to fewer friendship conflicts, more friendly competition and, for gifted students, greater friendship stability – a factor of vital importance since many gifted learners can struggle with this.

Differences between boys and girls

The interviews reveal that more boys than girls would say they are in it to win. Even parents, other than **Jess**'s, would say that their daughters are *"not overly-competitive"* or that they're *"competitive with self."* However, a study has shown that competitiveness due to gender is also task-

---

[76] Udvari, S.J. & Schneider, B.H. (2000) Competition and the Adjustment of Gifted Children: A Matter of Motivation. *Roeper Review* 22(4) 212-216.

[77] Schapiro, M., Schneider, B.H., Shore, B.M. & Margison, J.A. (2009) Competitive Goal Orientations, Quality and Stability in Gifted and Other Adolescents' Friendships: A Test of Sullivan's Theory About the Harm Caused by Rivalry. *Gifted Child Quarterly*, 53(2) 71-88.

sensitive.[78] When the competitiveness of one-hundred-and-twenty-nine students was examined in three different areas (motor, spatial, and verbal tasks), the results indicated that boys performed better than girls in the motor and spatial tasks while girls were more competitive than boys in the verbal tasks.

In the course of her interview **Olga**, aged twenty, said:

> *"I would consider myself competitive. With school results I wanted to be the best in the class. The advantage was that it motivated me and pushed me to do as well as I could. The disadvantage was that it put me in a position of comparing myself to others, and the disappointment that inevitably came with not being the best the whole time, which is impossible."*

As Olga indicates, competitiveness cannot be considered in isolation from self-esteem and the message it conveys to the self about the self. Common situations that present challenges related to cooperation and competition include working on group projects at school, coping with winning and losing games, dealing with performance fears, and coping with competition within families. **Rhys**, aged fifteen, said the most challenging aspect of school was working in groups where others wouldn't play their part.

Competition played a significant role in the learning and talent development of many of the gifted students interviewed. **Ethan**, a national sprinting and long jump champion, said: *"Athletics helped with my studies. The long jump showed me how to achieve the goals I set out for myself; I never half-do anything, I get a great sense of accomplishment. I was awarded a national prize for my secondary level exam results, and won a grant for six years. I was always in it to win."*

The number of gifted learners who were successful in competitive sport at a national or regional level was striking, and particularly in solo sports where they could be self-reliant. For example **Greg** "loved boxing" and now coaches professional boxers as a sports psychologist. **Jess** played tennis: *"I was the last player to make the team; became the number one player within a year."* And **Ava** is, as her mother says, *"very competitive with herself – all about winning – already earning seven golds out of eleven in national Taekwondo competitions. She excels at football too."*

---

78 Gindi, S., Kohan-Mass, J. & Pilipel, A. (2019) Gender Differences in Competition Among Gifted Students: The Role of Single-Sex Versus Co-Ed Classrooms. *Roeper Review* 41(3) 199-210.

Benefits of competition for gifted learners

Competition – whether in sports, academia or the arts – can show the gifted learner how to deal with both success and defeat. This is a valuable life skill. My experience of coaching teams was that frequently losing a match taught the students more than winning one. They needed each other for support, and it presented the teacher/coach with opportunities to impart important life lessons as you held them while they cried.

Competition can take place on a local football field, or at a chess club. School competitions are also good – essay contests, maths games, spelling bees. Psychiatric social worker Noreen Joslyn says: *"I have seen cases where gifted learners go off to college and basically fall apart academically when they see that there are many other high achievers like themselves."*[79] **Ethan** says: *"I am very competitive and would watch where I ranked in the class. I ranked in the ninetieth percentile in medicine, and was shocked that others whom I considered very good were only ranked in the thirty-third percentile."*

As parents and teachers, we need to stress that effort and persistence counts the most. Talking with the gifted learners about what they got out of a competition helps, whether they win or lose. **Rhys** says: *"I love competitions; I came third in a national chess competition. I enter quizzes too."* He adds that he is *"very competitive"*, and he encourages children to enter competitions. His mother agrees: *"Competitions provide Rhys with a challenge"* – a challenge he isn't getting via the curriculum.

Being able to handle cooperation and competition is an essential part of working and playing well with others.[80] However, gifted children often struggle with group activities. Their strong views about the 'right' way to do things (for example Jess's statement that "my way was always right") makes it hard for them to compromise. Their sensitivity about evaluations or fears of hurting others' feelings can lead them to avoid or overreact to even mild forms of competition. And because they're used to performing well, they may also find it hard to cope with setbacks, struggles or losses.

Still, research has shown that gifted students are inclined to favour competitive learning conditions over cooperative ones, which implies that certain levels of competitiveness are beneficial for performance.[81] Others say that competition is important for gifted children, but games should be carefully chosen to meet the needs of the specific group. Learners should be given the opportunity to play the same game several times, with a variety of partners, in order to develop more successful strategies.

---

79 Joslyn, N. (2022) *Gifted Kids and Competition*. Family Education [online].
80 Kennedy-Moore, E. (2012) *Helping Gifted Children Handle Cooperation and Competition*. Davidson Institute [online].
81 Li, A.K.F. & Adamson, G. (1992) Gifted Secondary Students' Preferred Learning Style: Cooperative, Competitive, or Individualistic? *Journal for the Education of the Gifted*, 16(1).

How to help – choosing games

Care should be taken when selecting appropriate games to ensure that the learning of the intended concepts is enhanced. For a game to be a useful educational tool, it should enable the student to increase their chances of improving their performance by developing a strategy.

☞ Cooperative games. Competition should be encouraged only when students are competing against their own standards or previous records or collaborating in a team. For this reason it is best to start with cooperative games that introduce an element of competition.

- 'Lavaland' team game for two teams:
  The objective is for the team to move from point A to point B using two yoga or gym mats, but the ground is lava so no one can touch it! The team must devise a strategy to move mats ahead while keeping everyone safe. If a team member touches the lava or comes off the mat, the team must start over again.

☞ Strategy games. Extending gifted students is a demanding task. Use strategy games (e.g. Mind Meister, Civilisation C, Neo K12 FlowChart Games) to develop higher-order thinking skills.[82] Follow up by tasking gifted students to create a challenging strategy game of their own.

☞ Science Olympiads. Provide high performers with opportunities for in-depth science learning. The Science Olympiads are a good example of differentiated education; they help refine participants' science-related interests and motivate them to pursue careers in the field. These activities can be pursued inside or outside school.

---

82 Cole, P. (2016) 10 Fun Web Apps, Games, for Teaching Critical Thinking Skills. EmergingEdTech [online].

Potential pitfalls of competition

Competition, if not handled well, can have negative impacts for the gifted. Because it is always associated with extrinsic motivation, it is regarded as having negative consequences for gifted students' creative endeavours, intrinsic motivation and acquisition of new skills.[83] Extreme competitiveness can also result in undue stress and anxiety.[84] **Jess** says: *"I always needed the hundred, the perfect score, sobbing if I got less and it took a lot of coaxing to convince me otherwise."* Her mother worried for her: *"Jess was very competitive and always wanted to win."* She said it was like the *"Jess show."*

> **Key Point**
>
> Competition, if not handled well, can have negative impacts for the gifted.

Competition in advanced performance plays a crucial role. Musically gifted students are more likely to experience competitive conditions compared with students in regular classes.[85] **Olga**'s mother noted this effect: *"Olga took pride in achieving the highest grades in her violin exams, but always played down school grades as a friend of hers bullied her about it. It ended badly with Olga very upset."* This highlights the need to also consider jealousy.[76] Parents and teachers should be aware that comparison can exacerbate the negative impacts of competition, in which individuals are motivated to emulate or outdo someone. It is better to encourage gifted learners to compare their own current and past performance for self-improvement. **Ava**'s teacher was aware of this: *"Ava was an all-rounder. I was conscious of over-praising her work in case of a backlash from fellow students."*

---

83 Ozturk, M. & Debelak, C. (2008) Affective Benefits from Academic Competitions for Middle School Gifted Students. *Gifted Child Today* 31(2).
84 Davis, G.A. & Rimm, S.B. (1985). *Education of the Gifted and Talented*. 5th ed. Pearson.
85 Kao, C.-Y. (2011) The dilemma of competition encountered by musically gifted Asian male students: An exploration from the perspective of gifted education. *High Ability Studies* 22(1) 19-42.

How to help – dealing with cooperation and conflict

Eileen Kennedy-Moore provides some useful advice to help gifted children handle cooperation and conflict.[80]

☞ Start by acknowledging your child's feelings. This helps them to feel understood and be more open to coping options. For example, you may say: "It's frustrating when you know how you want a project to go and the other kids don't take it seriously"; or "I understand you wish the teacher wouldn't compare you to your sister."

☞ Build up your child's tolerance for winning and losing by gradually exposing them to competition. The key to coping with competitive games is to realise that winning and losing are temporary states. Explain that we can't always win, and it would be no fun given how others would feel, but we can always participate by having a good time and enjoying other players' company. If a child is very sensitive, start with cooperative games. Move on to 'beat your own record' games, then short competitive games, then low threat 'kids against grown-ups' games. When the child is ready, participating in sports or other competitions can also encourage good sportsmanship.

☞ Encourage empathy. When gifted children focus completely on the result and ignore the process, they may disregard other children's feelings. Acknowledge your child's feelings first, then they may feel calm enough to consider others' reactions. You could ask questions, for example: "What did you notice about how Sarah was feeling during the argument?" and "How might you help her feel better?"

☞ Discuss what good process looks like. Children don't automatically know how to be a good sport. These are learned behaviours. Knowing what behaviours to aim for can make it more likely that they'll be able to practise them. Brainstorm ways to contribute to a group spirit – for example working without complaining, complimenting others, or asking others, "What game do you want to play?"

☞ Normalise performance anxiety. For many gifted children, fears about competition relate to performance anxiety. It's normal to want to avoid things that make us feel scared, but anxiety doesn't have to be a stop signal. Rather, it's a survival signal – our bodies' way of getting us ready to do something challenging. Too much anxiety can paralyse us, but research shows that the best performance tends to occur at moderate levels of anxiety. Discuss ways to manage anxiety at that level – for example visualisation, deep breathing, focusing on the task at hand and calming self-talk such as "I've done my revision and whatever comes up in this exam, I will handle it and do well."

☞ Instil a growth mindset. Gifted students are used to doing well, so they may feel at a loss if a sibling or peer performs better than they do. Or they may quickly decide that they're 'no good' at a task if they aren't instantly successful. Judgments such as "I'm good at maths and my sister is good at English" are dangerous. Steer them toward a growth mindset ("I'm getting better at English"). Help them embrace effort and stress that some areas of learning just take longer to master.

☞ Play the 'big or little' game. It's risky to attach one's self-worth to being better than anyone else. Help your child understand that comparisons are relative by discussing physical size: are they big or little? The answer is: bigger than a toddler and smaller than a teenager, but big enough for all their favourite activities. Is their bedroom big or little? It's bigger than a cupboard and smaller than a living-room, but big enough for all their things. So size is not a yes/no question, it's relative. The same is true for smartness. The important thing is that your child is smart enough to learn whatever they want to learn. Ask them: "What is it that you want to learn?" This is open-ended, about them and much more important than "Who is smartest?" With comparisons we always lose!

Chapter 16: Leadership

Our world, and our society, needs role models and leaders at local, national and international levels. Professions such as medicine, technology, industry, education, agriculture, politics and the arts need great minds – people who can use their intellect, creativity and critical judgment. Interest in leadership potential dates back to the time of the Ancient Greeks, and developing leadership among young people is of great interest among educators and leaders worldwide – especially as with advancing technologies, nations can be more connected than ever before and countries are becoming increasingly dependent upon each other in a global economy.

> *Expert View*
>
> *"The future belongs to you, but it can only belong to you if you participate and take charge"*
>
> Kofi Annan

The former Secretary-General of the United Nations, Kofi Annan, shared some instructive thoughts on leadership. He said:

> *"In an age of interdependence, global citizenship based on trust and sense of shared responsibility is a crucial pillar of progress. Business must work with governments and all other actors in society to mobilise global science, technology and knowledge to tackle the interlocking crises of hunger, disease, environmental degradation and conflict that are holding back the developing world."*

Gifted learners are a key part of the solution to this problem, and merit serious consideration and investment by governments, educators and parents alike. Increasingly, COVID-19 has shown us how interdependent we are, with the success of the developed world depending on how well we cooperate with the developing world. Consequently, countries need to produce leaders who are not only aware of national problems, but also prepared to address them and interested in making the world a better place for future generations.[86] Parents and educators have a crucial role to play in fostering the development of leadership skills in our gifted young people.

Despite being a designated talent area within the scope of gifted learners requiring a differentiated programme, leadership remains the least well-defined and least discussed of these curricular fields.[87] This chapter

---

86 Lee, S.-Y. & Olszewski-Kubilius, P. (2016) Leadership Development and Gifted Students. In R. J. R. Levesque (Ed.), *Encyclopedia of Adolescence*. Springer International Publishing.

87 Karnes, F.A. & Bean, S.M. (1990) *Developing Leadership in Gifted Youth*. ERIC Clearinghouse for Disabilities and Gifted Education [online].

considers the challenge of leadership from the perspective of the gifted learner. It considers the types of leadership styles evident among the gifted students interviewed, the leadership characteristics they display, their enormous interest in world problems and in communicating with adults, and the leadership difficulties that may be experienced by gifted youth.

What is leadership?

Leadership is the ability to influence the activities of an individual or group toward the achievement of a goal. The definition has evolved from the idea of someone being a 'born leader' or simply 'one who leads', to a more complex view of how a person exerts influence.[88] Both task-oriented and relationship-oriented leaders are necessary for effective group functioning, but the leadership abilities of either one of these categories of leaders may go unnoticed if the definition of leadership used by schools is one-dimensional. Educators and parents need to be aware of this.

Teachers working with gifted students may use these broadened notions of leadership to identify their strengths and weaknesses and use them as a framework for an intervention programme. As with creativity and thinking abilities, leadership skills can be developed and honed through training programmes. This is time and resources well spent for the young people themselves, as well as for society generally. If in doubt, consider those who believed in and invested in you when you were younger, and the impact that that has made in your life and your ability to give as a result.

Leadership characteristics and styles

Many characteristics demonstrated by gifted young people enable them to profit from leadership development.[95] They include the following, many of which we have already considered:

- The desire to be challenged
- The ability to solve problems creatively
- The ability to reason critically
- The ability to see new relationships
- Facility of verbal expression
- Flexibility in thought and action
- The ability to tolerate ambiguity
- The ability to motivate others

---

88 Addison, L. (1985). *Leadership Skills Among the Gifted and Talented*, 1985 Digest. ERIC Clearinghouse for Disabilities and Gifted Education [online].

In my interviews with gifted learners, their parents and their teachers, I asked if they showed the following six characteristics of leadership. These characteristics, as well as what are referred to as 'task-oriented' and 'relationship-oriented' leaders, are what we will consider here.

- Carries responsibility well
- Is sociable and outgoing
- Is self-confident with peers
- Is self-confident and communicates with adults in a mature way
- Has an interest in world problems and solving them
- Demonstrates honesty and transparency

Task-oriented leaders excel at establishing well-defined patterns of organisation, channels of communication and ways of getting things done. **Sabrina**'s teacher says: *"Group tasks fulfil her; she is involved in the charity club and takes it very seriously. She is very good in operations and implementation."* Sabrina concurs: *"I'm beginning to show leadership in class and am comfortable socially. I'm also strong linguistically."*

The relationship-oriented leader, on the other hand, leads by maintaining personal relationships with and between members of the group by opening up communication, providing emotional support and using facilitating behaviours. **Ruby** exemplifies this leadership style: *"Being head girl grounded me and gave me a sense of purpose. I would find it hard not to be leader of something; it comes easily to me, and I trust myself to do the best job."* This was noticed by her peers and secondary level teachers: *"Often people came to me with their problems. I have a good head on me. I was looked on as an adult although a child. A good gauge for teachers – they would check in with me to see if something was a good approach."*

This pattern of behaviour was evident in Ruby from an early age. Her reception teacher notes that *"her thought process was advanced and she understood the needs of the teacher almost as a peer. She was reliable and mature in her thoughts and reasoning."* Notably, Ruby said that she was also *"comfortable with taking on an isolated role in 'leadership' and didn't have to be in the mix"*, a sure sign of self-reliance and strong leadership.

The born leader

Ethan's primary teacher described him as *"a born leader"* who was sociable, outgoing, self-confident with peers and adults and very understanding of kids who didn't find learning easy. His mother agrees: "*Ethan knows how to work social situations.*" Similarly, **Melissa** was described as a "*great role model*" by her teacher. She was "*completely unaware of it, like a mature woman in the class – she had everyone with her but not in a power sense, it came naturally to her.*"

Melissa commented: "*I was sociable, self-confident, able to communicate, honest and upfront. I grew up in a house with so many adults. I got a lot of attention as a child. I grew to be quite intuitive – good at reading situations and people.*" The benefit of interviewing people like Melissa, now fifty-eight, is that we see how a gifted young person turned out as a mature adult: "*I loved my accountancy career and the people aspect of it. I particularly liked interviewing and mentoring trainees for the company. It was like a school.*"

The developing leader

Greg, a successful psychologist and popular motivational speaker, says he now demonstrates all the leadership qualities identified in the GLF: "*This is the person I've become*", he says. Jesus and his principles of "*love and kindness*" are his model. When in a dilemma he simply asks himself, "*What would Jesus do?*" His teacher said that he "*has the essence of realness at his core, a connection with his roots, heritage, and culture – this explains who you are.*" She added that his family "*understood teamwork before it was coined as a phrase – I saw him as a smart fellow with a good work ethic.*"

Emma's leadership gifts are emerging: "*I was shy in primary school*", she says, but she became more "*sociable and outgoing*" in secondary school. She has a "*big interest in history and is a member of a local historical society.*" She shocked her parents when she asked them to "*donate to a charity instead of giving her a Christmas present.*" Described by her teacher as "*very mature for her years*", Emma has a "*good circle of friends and sticks up for others if they are wrongly blamed.*"

Now a student of criminology at university, Emma is also invested in her own personal development: "*After study, to make time for myself, I read 'The Choice' by Edith Eger, a holocaust survivor.*" She has an excellent sense of perspective: "*I'm sure I have no stress at all compared with her.*"

Teachers and parents should recognise and affirm these emerging leadership styles in their gifted young people.

Communication and wider interests

It would be remiss of me not to comment on a singular stand-out characteristic that was present in every gifted learner I interviewed, namely the ability to communicate with adults in a mature way. This is an area in which **Olga**, for example, was *"different gravy"*, according to her school principal. I found the pattern fascinating. Parents and teachers should make the most of this quality for the benefit of the gifted young person.

The interviews also revealed that many gifted young people appear to have an innate interest in world problems and in solving them. At ten, **Nina** is keenly interested in history, a deep thinker and *"already proactive on social justice issues"*, according to her teacher. She believes in being *"accountable – she helps children in Yemen, wants to stop air pollution, and is interested in knowing how to be a good child."* Honest and transparent, her mother says she *"is finding her voice as a human rights advocate."*

Sasha, seventeen, is described by her teacher as having *"a humility; you could add twenty years to her age she is so mature."* Her goal is to pursue science and medicine to find cures for diseases. **Maria**, forty-two, would consider a career change: *"I would like to be doing something more meaningful than my job as an engineer."* A human rights advocate, she wants to *"make a small difference to the world in a sustainable way"*.

Leadership difficulties experienced by gifted young people

It was at times painful to hear of the difficulties experienced by gifted learners when they are motivated to make a difference but experience problems with communication and being understood, particularly when working in groups. Intellectually gifted young people generally enjoy working on their own, at their own pace, so a group setting can be quite testing for them. **Nina**'s mother would say that *"working in groups is very difficult for her; she is ignored by the other children, and she doesn't connect with them."* **Jude**, on the other hand, was sometimes a little too self-confident with peers due to his experiences as a prominent child actor: *"I feel different"* he said. *"He had to be taught to be aware of how he speaks with children"*, said his teacher.

Maria presented her difficult experience – queried as possibly having autism on a mild level, she said that *"communicating with others as an adult is difficult, the nuances and cues catch me."* She talks about coping strategies: *"I've had to learn to hide some things for self-protection. I feel taken for granted by others in organisations with respect to volunteering and activism due to my very high interest in human rights issues."* Her mother regrets the way life turned out for her daughter: *"At fifteen, she took on responsibility beyond her years when I separated from her father. She was inflexible and had difficulty with people, not learning. She was black and white in terms of communication – no middle ground, no savvy. She was honest to a fault."*

The difficult cases listed here show just how important it is for parents and teachers to mediate these situations for the wellbeing of their gifted child. While many gifted learners can and do function well in groups, it may need to be on the basis that they are allowed to assume a leadership role.

How to help – developing leadership abilities

Strategies for parents and caregivers:

- Help your child to see that a good leader lets others have ideas and input and doesn't make all the decisions. Highlight the differences between bossiness and cooperation, and teach them about the vital skills of listening, delegating, helping, facilitating and empathising.[89]

- Give your child opportunities to develop projects and take leadership responsibility from an early age. Gifted learners gain satisfaction and learn new skills by doing jobs for parents or teachers. For group tasks, let them come up with the roles and responsibilities they wish to take.

- Explain that we all develop at our own pace. This is a key lesson for children who may want to get everything right first time. Share examples of gifted learners' personal stories and leadership styles.

- Where feasible, take your child on visits to retirement homes to listen to and collect older people's stories. They can also do this with older relatives, capturing permanent family memories in the process.

- Gifted learners benefit from time spent with other gifted children. This can be achieved at school, but parents can also look at talent programmes and weekend and summer enrichment programmes.

---

[89] Webb, J.T., Gore, J.L. & Amend, E.R. (2007) *A Parent's Guide to Gifted Children*. Great Potential Press.

Strategies for teachers and schools:

☞ Education programmes should take a two-pronged approach to the development of leadership abilities in gifted students, by i. helping them to achieve leadership roles in their chosen fields and ii. nurturing those students identified as being generally gifted leaders.[97]

☞ Discuss leadership styles. Explain that 'active leaders' are influential through force of personality, while 'reflective leaders' exert influence through the impact of their ideas. Empower learners by explaining that they can be leaders in their own gifted area by contributing ideas.

☞ Emphasise the importance of continuous self-development and reading as a leader. Highlight that successful leaders are always open to new approaches to making an impact and developing as people.

☞ Give gifted students opportunities to discuss the difficulties of working in groups. Ask them what is easy and hard about groupwork and ask them to devise an approach to make it more effective.

☞ Encourage gifted students to propose responses to issues of local, national and global interest (e.g. climate change). Be a sounding board for their ideas and steer them towards an agreed course of action.

Part 5: Social and emotional development

Chapter 17: Self-esteem and acceptance

Self-esteem is the degree to which we know, value and like ourselves as individuals. It is a feeling of self-worth and positivity, leading to the belief that we can feel loved and fulfil our life purpose. It is ultimately about self-acceptance, that we are 'good enough'. Self-esteem is a fragile flower, and one that can be built or broken at any time, so we must tread carefully.

> **Key Point**
>
> *Self-esteem is a fragile flower, and one that can be built or broken at any time, so we must tread carefully.*

With that said, a good foundation in the early years helps immensely. This is true for all children, but especially the gifted child. Yet, with help and patience, the gifted child can develop a healthy level of self-esteem whereby they not only feel accepted but also learn to accept themselves.

So self-esteem is crucially important for the gifted learner. Susan Daniels and Michael Piechowski suggest that, for gifted children, "Life is experienced in a manner that is deeper, more vivid, and more acutely sensed."[90] Of course, low social self-esteem is by no means just a problem for gifted children, but it can manifest differently and more intensely in them. Complicating matters still further, because competence and achievement are generally thought to be key elements of self-esteem and are intertwined with a child's evaluation of his or her own self-worth, people may mistakenly assume that competent, high-achieving learners must be exempt from low self-esteem.[91] They are not, and this is a very real danger for gifted children.

The needs of gifted learners

Understanding the complexity of the emotional, social and relationship needs of gifted children, along with their ramifications, is not easy. So much depends on the understanding and skillset of the educators and teachers that gifted children meet. In personal conversation with Early Years educator Hazel Murphy about the giftedness of the young child, she said: "They bring their gift into the classroom if you let them. We always wanted it to remain a gift, we never wanted it to become an affliction."

---

90 Daniels, S. & Piechowski, M.M. (2009) *Living with Intensity: Understanding the Sensitivity, Excitability, and Emotional Development of Gifted Children, Adolescents and Adults*. Gifted Unlimited.

91 Meyers, L. (2014) Gifted Children: Not immune to low self-esteem. *Counseling Today* [online].

How fortunate for those gifted children – she recognised their gifts and welcomed their differences in the classroom.

No one claims that catering for the gifted learner is an easy responsibility, however. Gifted children's individual emotional, social and relational experiences deserve to be catered for in specific ways that will enable them to not only make progress but to enjoy their educational experiences and develop interpersonal relationship abilities that will benefit them over the course of their lives."[92] Hence, our goal as parents and educators should be to empower the child to accept themselves for who they are, and, critically, to facilitate their acceptance by others. A child may be aware that their gifts may set them apart, but that doesn't mean that they shouldn't be happy or feel a valued part of their school community.

Maria had a difficult childhood and found making friends hard. Neither she nor her mother could nominate a teacher to be interviewed for this book – she felt that she never had a teacher who 'got' her. She is now forty-one and, regrettably, low self-esteem has permeated her life: *"I feel like I've been firefighting most of my life. I don't have good boundaries. My needs are put right at the end."* Friendship challenges persist: "I make friends but keep them at a superficial level, and I feel guilty not having more contact. I've fallen out with friends along the way too." She shares her view of the problem: *"I haven't learned some of the relational skills. Communication can be awkward, for example – understanding banter, the subtleties."*

Early years education

Research has shown that it is critical to identify the gifted child as early as possible, before they feel too different, isolated or misunderstood. Young and gifted children often exhibit a higher level of maturity than their peers in one or more areas of development.[93] This maturity is associated with a number of intellectual skills – for example advanced verbal ability, reading ability, mathematical ability, time perception, memory retention, attention span. To further complicate formal identification, high ability in one area may co-exist with ordinary ability in another. Louise Porter believes that gifted children as young as two years old may know that they are different, and she argues that they deserve an explanation for their differences to avoid potential issues such as low self-esteem.[94]

---

92 Delaune, A. (2016). Emotional, social, and relationship development for gifted and talented children in early childhood education. *He Kupu*, 4.

93 Kuo, C.-C., Maker, J., Su, F.-L. & Hu, C. (2010) Identifying young gifted children and cultivating problem solving abilities and multiple intelligences. *Learning and Individual Differences* 20(4) 365-379.

94 Porter, L. (2005) Young Gifted Children: Meeting Their Needs. Early Childhood Australia Research in Practice Series, 12 (3).

The interviews revealed that social, emotional and relational issues were often the challenges that tested the gifted learners the most. **Nina**'s teacher explains her situation: "*At eight she was very down, a very young age. To help her I started a diary for her thoughts and feelings to stop her 'over-thinking'. She loosened up a little when she knew she could come to talk to me, I encouraged her not to be afraid to be different, and so did her mother. When she was hard on herself, I intervened and offered her a different role. There was also a tendency for Nina to be teased by other children, for example when she dressed up as a suffragette.*"

Nina herself says: "*I don't really fit in with the girls in my class; all I want is a little friend like me, a girl that would like history and want to be friends and look out for me.*" Similarly, fifteen-year-old **Amy** says she "*feels awkward sometimes*." Her mother describes her as "*nerdy*" but says that she copes by "*finding friends like herself*." It is difficult to hear how alienated young and gifted children like Nina and Amy can feel in class. They can depend hugely on others for support. "*She would perk up when I'd recognise her in the line in the morning*", said Nina's teacher. Cases like these show that gifted learners need validation for who they are in their own right – to know that their differences are accepted and, above all, that they belong.

The challenge for parents

If I were to sum up in a single sentence my experience of interviewing the parents of gifted learners, I would say that they are often their children's saviours. Most of them made sacrifices – such as Nina's mother who gave up her job as a social worker to be available to debrief her daughter after school from the age of six, **Dylan**'s mother who got outside help including play therapy and private educators to support her with a "*socially frustrated*" son, and **Lucy**'s mother who recognised her baby's sensory difficulties, changed the home routine and undertook sensory training to help her child. To their credit, all the parents I interviewed saw their child's differences and did their best to adapt.

It isn't always easy, though. Despite the rhetoric of partnership, the reality is that parents of pupils with special educational needs (including giftedness) often report that their relationships with school staff and other professionals are characterised by stress, frustration and alienation.[95] Some are even considered to be 'bragging'. Parents who try to advocate for their children so as to develop their abilities may even find themselves in conflict with teachers, the school and the educational system, whose

---

95 Porter, L. (2020). *Gifted Young Children: A guide for teachers and parents*. Routledge.

agenda is for an egalitarian approach, even when articulating a discourse of collaboration.[96]

Parental expectations and barriers to participation should always be considered when thinking about and planning for the gifted learner. Encouragement should be given to facilitate parental involvement in the interests of their gifted son or daughter. Other family members shouldn't be forgotten either. The long-range observations by significant others such as grandparents can provide the information needed to clarify the nature and levels of a child's talents and help pave the way to more effective educational planning and services. [97]

Self-criticism

As we have noted, friendship challenges can make acceptance and self-acceptance difficult for gifted students. Gifted learners can also be overly self-critical in evaluating and correcting their own efforts, and in setting unrealistically high standards for themselves (two of the points mentioned in the 'Self-esteem' section of the GLF). **Amy** is *"overly self-critical with tests and results"* and says: *"I hold myself to high standards."* Her mother observed that *"she goes off and studies on her own, is really concerned about poor standards – she wouldn't give herself enough credit."* **Ethan** says: *"I was tough on myself; overly self-critical."* His mother agreed: *"he'd say, 'I did badly in that test', but he would ace it."* Now midway through a medicine degree, Ethan says: "I acknowledge limitations only now."

Jess's mother described her as having a *"tough exterior but a very sensitive interior"*, and says that she set *"unrealistic standards; always overly self-critical."* **Sasha** enjoys *"self-acceptance and ease"* but is intense: *"If I want ninety and get eighty-eight, I'm hard on myself even-though I'm close."* Her father agrees: *"She cares, works hard, and is nearly traumatised with hard marks – a teacher pleaser. She sets the bar too high."*

Interestingly, none of these four gifted learners had friendship issues – but all four were tough on themselves emotionally. They used exam results as the bar against which they measured their worth. Writing about her own gifted daughter, the teacher, author and advocate Cindi Rigsbee confirms this pattern: "Her 'invisible standards' were difficult to address since they resulted from her 'own expectations'. My words of

---

96 Silverman, L.K., & Golon, A.S. (2008) Clinical Practice with Gifted Families. In Pfeiffer, S.I. (Ed.), *Handbook of Giftedness in Children: Psychoeducational Theory, Research, and Best Practices*. Springer.

97 Feldhusen, J. (2001) Through Another's Eyes: The Role of Grandparents in Talent Recognition and Development. *Gifted Child Today* 24(3) 25-65.

comfort were never as loud as her 'inner voice'."[98] For Cindi's daughter, and for many other gifted students like her, the extreme pressure they experience comes not from outside, but from within – from their own inner self-critic.

How to help – self-esteem

Strategies for parents and caregivers:

☞ Children's books can be wonderful tools to start a conversation about self-esteem. Good examples are *I Am Enough*, suitable for primary students and filled with positive affirmations,[99] and *I Am Perfectly Designed*, for anyone who has ever felt different or not good enough.[100]

☞ Seek opportunities for your child to meet other gifted children so they develop a healthy sense of self rather than an inflated ego. Gifted and talented groups may offer social opportunities at their intellectual level.

☞ The messages we tell ourselves matter, and we all need reminding of the power of positive self-talk. Share affirmations, and encourage your child to 'collect' nice things that people say about them – useful to refer to when their self-critic emerges.

☞ Provide creative, non-competitive outlets for your child – for example painting or playing a musical instrument for enjoyment. Activities that bring joy without pressure are positive diversions for gifted children.

☞ Supportive communication from parents can offer encouragement and open up dialogue. Leave a sticky note in your child's lunchbox, send a supportive text, or look for other ways to encourage them.

---

98 Rigsbee, C. (2018) *Strategies for Helping Stressed-Out Gifted Learners*. Teacher's Workshop [online].
99 Byers, G. & Bobo, K.A. (2020) *I Am Enough*. BalzerBray.
100 Brown, K., Brown, J. & Syed, A. (2020) *I Am Perfectly Designed*. Macmillan.

Strategies for teachers and schools:

☞ Teach the 'Five Building Blocks of Self-Esteem' to spark discussion about self-image, feelings and understanding.[101] The five blocks are a sense of identity, belonging, security, competence and purpose. Use them to explore how students might cope in various 'what if?' scenarios.

☞ Normalise feelings that learners may consider negative such as anger, jealousy or hatred. Help students understand that they are not bad for having such feelings – what matters is how they respond to them. ARC is a good approach to practise – **a**ccept, **r**elease, offer self-**c**ompassion.

☞ Instil a growth mindset by stressing that while gifted students may be great at one subject, this may not apply to all subjects. It is likely to be news to the gifted learner that grades do not make a good person, and that we are all on our own individual journey of growth.

☞ Give students the opportunity to talk through their feelings. Gifted learners can be very sensitive to 'letting their parents down', and a teacher can give them space they don't permit themselves at home.

☞ Discuss how thoughts lead to feelings (e.g. thinking about the moon generates wonder; a lost pet generates sadness), then explain that it is possible to change how we feel by changing our thoughts (CBT).

☞ Design activities to ensure gifted learners are valued and included. Because they often excel at intellectual challenges like quizzes and spelling, other children often want them on their teams. This can positively change the class dynamic.

---

[101] Borba, M. (1989) Esteem Builders. A K-8 *Self- Esteem Curriculum for Improving Student Achievement, Behavior and School Climate*. Jalmar Press

Chapter 18: Perfectionism

Perfectionism is a multi-dimensional personality disposition that is characterised by relentless striving for high personal standards, overly critical self-evaluation, judging self-worth based on one's ability to achieve these unrelenting standards, and persisting despite negative consequences and high personal cost.[102] Perfectionism is frequently highlighted as a core characteristic of intellectually gifted students, and unsurprisingly it is one of the most common concerns among parents and teachers.[103]

> *Key Point*
>
> Perfectionism is a core characteristic of intellectually gifted students, and one of the most common concerns among parents and teachers.

This chapter explores the perfectionist trait of gifted children. For some gifted learners, perfectionism actually becomes a form of self-abuse, leading to paralysis and discontent. As we shall see, often the solution to personal happiness is finding the means to let go of that idea of perfection, creating the freedom to flourish and realise the real essence of one's gift.

Healthy and unhealthy perfectionism

Perfectionism is often seen as wanting to be perfect or do something perfectly. But there is a big difference between a healthy, helpful pursuit of continuous improvement and an unhealthy, unhelpful quest for perfection. Healthy perfectionism is setting realistic goals and standards in a way that makes you more likely to achieve those goals and experience a sense of fulfilment, whereas unhealthy perfectionism is taking it to the point of feeling frustrated and blaming yourself for not doing everything perfectly.

Characteristics of perfectionism include:

- Difficulty making decisions
- Reassurance-seeking
- Excessive organising
- Giving up too soon for fear of failure
- Procrastination
- Not knowing when to stop

---

[102] CCI (2019) *Perfectionism in Perspective*. Centre for Clinical Interventions [online].
[103] Wilson, H.E. & Adelson, J.L. (2018). Perfectionism: Helping Gifted Children Learn Healthy Strategies and Create Realistic Expectations. *Parenting for High Potential*, 7(3), 8.

- Correcting things and/or others
- Over-compensating
- Repeatedly checking
- Hoarding
- Failure to delegate
- Avoidance
- Slowness, for example speaking slowly so you say the right thing

For gifted young perfectionists, learning when to stop and let themselves off the hook is crucial. Quite a number of the learners interviewed had perfectionist tendencies. For example, **Miguel**, forty, said *"I'm intense, want things to be right"*, and his mother said that in secondary school *"he would re-do his work."* **Emma**, nineteen, said: *"If I got 90% for a history essay, I'd want to know how I could have got the extra marks."* Others were more extreme; for example ten-year-old **Lucy** said: *"I could spend four or five hours doing a painting. If there was a little patch not right and I couldn't fix it perfectly, I would re-do the whole thing – the extra hours didn't matter."*

Although at twenty-four **Ruby** is quite self-aware, she is confused by the paradox of perfectionism. *"I'm guilty of toxic perfectionism. I recognise it but find it hard to unravel. It pays off a lot of the time, but it has stunted me as well. I won't engage if I can't do something perfectly – for example, I'd choose not to sing a song unless my voice would do it perfectly. Musician friends say I need to loosen up. Sometimes it's worth doing what they say – it's only me that notices the blip!"* Reflecting, she says *"it's not easy knowing I won't be best at everything, realising there is no such thing as the true perfect. I also procrastinate, leaving things till I'm under pressure."*

Ruby's mother outlined typical characteristics: *"She will keep going forever until someone says stop! She is afraid to push herself out of her comfort zone for fear of failure. Fear of performing could manifest as a cough – trying to find a reason why her performance wouldn't be perfect. She doesn't like things not to turn out as planned."* Ruby explains: *"approval from my parents is still important to me – I always try to make a good impression."* She adds: *"I need to be brought down to earth. Realising your reputation is only in your own head and not taking myself too seriously helps me."*

The value of mistakes

Some gifted students actually believe that their perfectionism is a good thing. When asked 'Has your giftedness changed over time?', **Ava** said: *"I've started to get better, more intense, as I get older with it getting more* *difficult to maintain the 'A' grades. It's what I want and work for."* And **Ethan**, twenty-three, simply replied: *"My perfectionism is getting better."* Gifted learners such as Ava and Ethan may benefit from learning the value of making mistakes. Not being afraid to make mistakes releases some of the pressure of perfectionism, and allows the learner to go into uncharted waters where they may discover their real genius.

A good way to approach this is to suggest that gifted learners make a list of five mistakes that they made recently, along with what they learned about themselves and whether it changed a core belief.

Mistakes I made	What I learned about myself	Did you change a core belief? If so, what is your new belief?
1.		
2.		
3.		
4.		
5.		

The 'perfectionism loop'

Ava, fifteen, is caught in a vicious cycle of self-imposed expectations. *"I really like the best standard of work I can produce; if not I'm disappointed with myself."* The expectation of 'exceptional' work *"can be pressure – I do study a lot and may put in more effort than others because I want to achieve, I expect it of myself."* Her teacher identified perfectionism as the problem: *"Ava's work was never good enough in her own eyes. Her homework was meticulous – spending two-and-a-half hours per night in primary school. She achieved full marks everywhere but in her self-assessment she rated herself 7/10 saying 'maybe my homework could be better'!"*

Ava's perfectionism is becoming more embedded and intense as she gets older, a recognisable pattern among 'gifted perfectionist' learners. At the time of our interview, she had already spent four hours doing homework after a half-day in school. Her mother worries: *"She has an addiction to perfection and homework. Her perfectionism showed at two years old – she wouldn't colour over lines even then! Our family walk is now missed in favour of homework."* She shared her concern about the practicalities of life: *"The gap is enormous between Ava's intellect and her savviness."*

Clearly, perfectionism becomes a vicious circle for some gifted learners. The affirmation they receive for great work gets mixed-up along the way with the core of their self-esteem. To maintain their high standards and keep achieving high marks they work even harder to meet their own expectations. They are their own hardest critic. These gifted learners are essentially in a 'perfectionism loop' and don't know how to escape. They will benefit from knowing and practising the difference between healthy and unhealthy perfectionism, and from recognising the value of mistakes.

How to help – perfectionism

Strategies for parents and caregivers:

☞ Some gifted children get the idea that if they're smart, everything will come easy. This makes them more likely to give up if something is hard. Remind them that even the best performers practise a lot and help them to develop a manageable plan for overcoming obstacles.

☞ Recognise your child's gift but don't generalise and expect top marks in all areas. Being 'smart' brings pressure – explain that they can't be great at everything. Share stories of famous people – for example Einstein was a gifted scientist, but that didn't mean that he was a gifted composer too.

☞ Discuss why failure is okay, exploring the personal learning involved. Deal with our shaming culture – the shame of failing and its impact on wellbeing. Share great stories of resilience and individuals 'bouncing back'.

☞ Watch for changing behaviour such as deepening intensity, isolation or self-criticism. Sometimes, even with support, a gifted learner may need help to deal with low self-worth. Seek counselling if required.

☞ Help your child to recognise their contributions to all areas of life, not just academia. Encourage them to create a list of accomplishments that they are proud of. You can start them off, and do the same yourself.

Strategies for teachers and schools:

☞ Take time to listen to students' core beliefs. Often, they can't forgive themselves for not being perfect, and believe that they've let others down. Validate their feelings, explain the difference between healthy and unhealthy perfectionism, observe them and help them break the 'perfectionism loop'.

☞ Teach students that mistakes can be good. A willingness to make mistakes prevents self-worth being tied solely to achievement and allows the individual to be separated from their effort and results.

☞ Enable gifted children to help themselves. Encourage them to use their many capabilities to solve their problems and to obtain a balanced view of self-worth in social and intellectual contexts.

☞ Use portfolios to assess gifted learners' work. This is one of my preferred approaches to assessing the perfectionist. By looking at samples of their work over time, you can have a genuine conversation about problems, progress and growth.

☞ Adopt a light-hearted approach if learners take themselves too seriously. This grounds them and helps them to let go of the issue. Draw on the ARC approach (**a**cceptance, **r**elease, self-**c**ompassion).

Chapter 19: Over-excitability and intensity

The concept of over-excitability (OE) in gifted students has been validated across several research studies.[104] Over-excitability may be defined as an inborn, higher-than-average capacity for experiencing inner and external stimuli, and higher than average responsiveness in the nervous system. Kazimierz Dabrowski (1902-1980), a Polish psychiatrist and psychologist, developed the theory of over-excitabilities across five specific areas.[105] While not all gifted learners have OEs, there are more people with OEs in the gifted population than in the general population. Dabrowski observed that innate ability combined with OE was predictive of high potential.

> *Expert View*
>
> "My mind is always racing, and always going and always working, and it's a gift and a curse."
>
> Sean Combs (Puff Daddy)

The five areas of over-excitability are:

- Psychomotor – an abundance of physical energy, often manifested as a liking for sporting activities
- Sensual – heightened responses of the senses and aesthetic appreciation
- Imaginational – a capacity for fantasy
- Intellectual – curiosity, aliveness of the mind
- Emotional – sensitivity, intensity, empathy

Studies have revealed that gifted learners show proven differences on the over-excitability scale; and have also demonstrated a positive correlation between over-excitability and perfectionism. There are gender differences too, with higher parental expectations and concern over mistakes in female students. Male students tend toward the psychomotor over-excitement type; the emotional type is more prevalent among female students.

Gifted learners can be extremely sensitive in one or more of the five areas above, meaning that they react more strongly and for longer than normal to a stimulus that may be very small. **Ava** was described by her mother as:

---

104 Silverman, L.K. (2012). *Giftedness 101*. Springer Publishing Company.
105 Tolan, S.S. (1999). *Dabrowski's Over-excitabilities: A Layman's Explanation*. Hoagies' Gifted Education [online].

"intense, over-excitable – acquires a lot of attention, very expressive, loud, highly communicative child, not a TV person, up and walking around, needs to know what's ahead." The response involves psychological factors and a heightened level of central nervous system sensitivity.

Intensity

Often due to the prevalence of these over-excitabilities, gifted children tend to be more intense in their feelings.[106] This can cause them either to stand out or to try to be unnoticed, making them easy targets for teasing and bullying. A further factor contributing to the intensity observed in gifted learners may be that it is a result of these young people internalising the message that it is not okay for them to be who they really are. This can damage their self-esteem, and lead to heightened intensity.[107]

Lucy is an example of an individual demonstrating extreme sensual over-excitability and intensity. She has physical sensitivities such as extremely sensitive skin, and she was a difficult baby to pacify with allergies to wheat, dairy and yeast. Her mother explains: *"I noticed she was different when she was a baby' – super-sensitive. The amount of information that went in was overload, she was over-sensitive to her environment, born with a higher stress level. Super-sensitive to noises like hair dryers, vacuum cleaners, thunder. I couldn't take her to the supermarket or the library – high ceilings had low vibrations – she was hearing stuff nobody else could hear. I had to hold her differently, but not tightly – her arms and legs had to be free."*

She explains their solution: *"We had to alter our world to find ways to relieve her pain as a baby. We also had to educate our two older daughters, as Lucy was getting all the attention."* She continues: *"We had a breakthrough when Lucy was three and a half – I found a sound therapy/listening programme to calm her stress responses. Sensory processing was a game-changer – I gave her sensory experiences like a trampoline, a gym-mat, sand and water, all in our living-room, and she went to these areas as she needed them. Sometimes I had to say to Lucy: 'I can't hear the sounds you hear or feel the lumps you feel on the couch, you'll have to sort it yourself.'"*

Lucy acknowledges her sensitivities: *"Open-heart meditation really helped calm my body/eczema with the sensitivities I have."*[108] Her mother cautions that *"children who are super-sensitive go into shame quicker than others."*

---

106 Thompson-Kroon, J.E. (2011) Defining Reality: The Parental Experience of Getting to a Diagnosis of Asperger Syndrome. PhD thesis, Gannon University.
107 LaChance, N. (2016). *Social Self-Esteem and Gifted Kids*. Institute for Educational Advancement [online].
108 www.openheartmeditation.com/

Dylan experiences intellectual and imaginational over-excitability: His teacher said: *"Before a violin concert, he would be up to ninety. He is a perfectionist – he visualises what he wants to create and then follows through to the letter of the law. If it doesn't work out, he can explode. For example, making a Halloween mask, a parent had to come to his rescue."* Dylan is intense. His mother said: *"He needs to be kept stimulated, and he would play video games all day if he was allowed to. That would be disastrous for him. He'll push against all boundaries, he can come home from school in a foul mood, he needs to decompress and be listened to. He's really highly-strung, and he needs a solid home routine – a good diet, sleep and quiet time are all important for him."*

How to help – over-excitability and intensity

Strategies for parents and caregivers:

☞ The body needs to be calm before the brain can work well. Provide sensory experiences such as a trampoline, a gym-mat and a swing. Long baths, playing in mud, sand and water all help. Routine at home is also important – a good diet, quiet time and sleep matter.

☞ Be a sounding board when things go wrong. Recognise when your child is too far gone emotionally to help themselves, and know that they will need more listening and reassurance than other children.

☞ Be there, calm and steady, when emotional outbursts occur. Do not make light of it, and seek to bridge the gap between the gifted child undergoing an outburst and other people who may not understand.

☞ Accept your child's differences as part of who they are, and help them develop a sense of themselves as valued members of the community.

Strategies for teachers and schools:[102]

☞ Provide rich language to aid the young gifted learner. Move beyond the basic 'happy, sad, angry' to more advanced vocabulary. This allows them to better express the nuances in their emotions and maintain relationships with others as they describe how they are feeling.

☞ Awareness of sensitivities aids understanding of learners' responses to specific situations. If a child covers their ears, they may have a sensitivity to noise. Ensure they feel safe, and find out what works.

See the whole child. It is essential that the individual is always the primary consideration, without fragmenting their giftedness, isolating their emotional sensitivity or assuming that it implies vulnerability.

 Ensure that gifted learners are not seen as 'whiney' members of the class – this will set the tone for other children's behaviour, and aid emotional regulation.

Chapter 20: Stress and anxiety

Gifted students are much more than their impressive test scores. It can be difficult to see past their potential, and glimpse the young person who may be anxious, lonely, confused or unsure of what the future might bring.[109] For some gifted children, such feelings are very real, and for them to become healthy adults it is vital that they be identified at an early age, that they receive

> ## Key Point
> It can be difficult to see past the gifted student's potential, and glimpse the young person who may be anxious, lonely, confused or unsure.

appropriate education, that support and counselling are provided for emotional needs, and that parents and teachers are fully informed. This chapter reviews some key literature on the psychological wellbeing of gifted learners and examines a tendency to be prone to worry and anxiety.

Personality theorists have long suggested that the management of anxiety plays a primary role in positive adjustment, and that it is essential for teachers and parents to acknowledge the added complexity facing gifted individuals.[110] A possible explanation for this is that although all children face anxiety, the gifted must often deal with it at an earlier age than other children. Gifted children's anxiety may also be significantly shaped by the acceptance they receive for their unique abilities and the coping skills they learn and are able to use. Anxiety may also accumulate and manifest during adolescence, with the individual becoming more intense and perfectionist over time.[111]

There is a long history of studies examining how giftedness influences the psychological well-being of individuals. Maureen Neihart points out that there is evidence to support two contrasting views – firstly that giftedness enhances resilience in individuals, and secondly that giftedness increases vulnerability. Differences arise because psychological well-being is multi-dimensional and gifted learners are a diverse group. Significantly, whether psychological outcomes for gifted individuals are positive or negative

---

[109] Galbraith, J. & Delisle, J. (2015) *When Gifted Kids Don't Have All the Answers: How to Meet Their Social and Emotional Needs*. Free Spirit Publishing.
[110] Bradley, T. (2006) *Chill Out: Helping Gifted Youth Deal with Stress*. TerryBradleyGifted [online].
[111] Dirkes, M.A. (1983) Anxiety in the gifted: Pluses and minuses. *Roeper Review* 6(2) 68-70.

seems to depend on at least three factors that interact synergistically: firstly the type of giftedness, secondly the educational fit (or lack of it), and thirdly the individual's own personal characteristics.[112]

Childhood experiences and development

In early childhood years, gifted children's emotional development is often advanced. However, the effects of this advanced development upon the gifted child's social and relationship development may vary.[102] Childhood experiences matter a great deal. **Maria**, now forty-one, says she *"didn't have emotionally available parents."* Her father had serious mental health difficulties and her mother *"went to pieces"* after a baby's cot death when Maria was just three. Her mother agrees: *"As a young child, Maria didn't have an easy life. Her Dad and I separated when she was fifteen and she took on responsibilities beyond her years… being the eldest she took the brunt."* She continues: *"Due to our sudden exit from the family home, Maire had no textbooks for three months and she still got straight A's in her exams. There were times when she was desperately unhappy in school, and she needed extra help with the social dimension."* Maria openly admits that she still struggles today with personal challenges.

Many gifted children develop an early awareness for issues of justice and a concern for the well-being of others. They tend to ask questions about right and wrong, and about death and the possibility of life beyond, and they often take an interest in philosophy and social issues.[100] However, some of them pay a high price for this advanced moral development and high moral code. **Dylan**'s sense of justice *"overwhelms any personal sense of self-preservation"*, says his mother. Dylan himself explains: *"It's like OCD – I want everything to fit in neatly. I'm over-critical – I feel compelled to tell others if they're doing something wrong, and then I get into trouble."*

The impact of the 'gifted label'

Being identified as gifted can have a significant impact on the mental wellbeing of a child. Research has shown that children whose parents used the label 'gifted' are more likely to report adjustment difficulties than those whose parents do not.[113] Dr David Garner suggests that early labelling of children as gifted may increase parental expectations for

---

[112] Neihart, M. (2011) *The Impact of Giftedness on Psychological Well-Being*. SENG [online].
[113] Cornell, D.G. (1989) Child Adjustment and Parent Use of the Term "Gifted". *Gifted Child Quarterly* 33(2).

performance, contributing to perfectionist behaviours.[114] Further, parents may overvalue their gifted child and intensify the child's expectations to meet parental needs, which can create problems during adolescence such as the 'perfectionist loop' described in Chapter 18.

The images of mentally disturbed gifted individuals that permeate society have an impact upon gifted individuals too. This perception is unhelpful and should be counteracted at every level. In the interview case studies, some parents chose to send their children to 'gifted' enrichment outreach programmes and found them quite helpful – but others chose not to, even when they were invited to do so. Instead, partly because they felt that being labelled 'gifted' was a concern, they opted to accommodate their child's additional needs privately or in collaboration with schools.

Anxiety and its risks

All children are susceptible to worry and anxiety, to a greater or lesser extent depending on their circumstances and characteristics. This risk can increase dramatically during the adolescent years, when worries about school, exams and the future can become all-pervasive. The interviews bear this out. **Amy**, fifteen, gets *"anxious about tests."* **Emma**, nineteen, said *"I worry when I take into consideration the life purpose of school."* And **Sasha**, seventeen, said: *"I worry about tests even after they're over. Worry then spills over into day-to-day life."*

Sabrina, fifteen, experiences anticipatory anxiety: *"I get too worked-up about exams although I do quite well."* Her mother agrees: *"Sabrina has performance anxiety – crying, panic attacks."* **Olga** recalls a pattern: *"At ten I was super-stressed for violin exams, crying, not being able to sleep, self-critical. Before my final exams I was a stress-ball. So much public discourse finally got to me, and I wasn't able to concentrate. The doctor prescribed relaxants which helped."* When I asked Olga what the worry was that underpinned the stress she said: *"Fear of failure; all the work for nothing; letting my parents down; didn't want to fall at the last hurdle."*

Jess, twenty-nine, said: *"Every test and every score that wasn't perfect worried me. I was devastated when I didn't get into medical school. I was in the top ten wait list. I had done everything, got top scores, head of every club."* She talks about recovering: *"In college I changed; I did more social stuff with friends. I still wanted to do well but I learned that I didn't need to be perfect, and I relaxed eventually. Even now as a new mom I can be unrealistically perfectionist – the first three years of a child's life are the most important!"*

---

114 Garner, D. (1991) Eating disorders in the gifted adolescent. In Bireley, M. & Genshaft, J. (1991) *Understanding the Gifted Adolescent* pp. 50-64. Teacher's College Press.

Studies have shown that during adolescence some gifted students relieve pressures through withdrawal or overt rejection of adult values. They may become under-achievers or drop out.[116] A recent study also concluded that gifted children are at risk of poor mental health.[115] Some studies indicate a link between high intellectual functioning and eating disorders, with perfectionism, competitiveness and high performance expectations from the self and others all viewed as possible contributors to their onset.[116] With creative adults, higher rates of mood disorders and suicide were revealed among gifted writers and visual artists in the pursuit of exceptional artistic achievement. Teachers and parents therefore need to be alert to the vulnerability that may be associated with creative talent.

How to help – countdown to exams

Gifted learners can worry incessantly about exams. An organised routine is key to reducing stress and exhaustion during the final few weeks.

- Have a master revision plan for each subject – control the controllable!

- Prioritise by asking your subject teachers' advice about key topics or chapters you need to prioritise for study.

- Advance plan: make selections for your daily revision plan in advance from your master plans.

- Practise smart time management – plan your time in hourly or half-hourly chunks (including a break) for optimal results. Check out the pomodoro technique (a time management method).

- Ensure you have adequate water, food, rest and daily exercise, and seek family support in ensuring that you maintain this.

- Study your daily plan as you've laid it out – structure is good!

- Use past exam papers to check how questions were presented previously – this increases confidence.

- Summarise: highlight key points in summaries and teacher notes.

---

115 Eren, F., Çete, A.Ö., Avcil, S. & Baykara, B. (2018) Emotional and Behavioral Characteristics of Gifted Children and Their Families. *Archives of Neuropsychiatry* 55(2) 105-112.

116 Dally, P. & Gomez, J. (1979) Capgras: Case study and reappraisal of psychopathology. *British Journal of Medical Psychology* 52(3) 291-295.

☞ Learn in a way that works for you – you'll know more than you think!

☞ Work out ways to help you remember your key points – acronyms, mnemonics and other memory aids can help.

☞ Manage your thoughts – stay in the here and now, and don't worry about the results of the exam before you sit it![117]

Educational fit

Appropriate educational provision for gifted students was emphasised consistently by the parents and teachers interviewed. **Luka**'s mother recalled that in primary school there was pressure to conform: *"Luka felt singled out by a teacher who was overly focused on sports, which was not Luka's thing."* However, there is a level of IQ at which it becomes very difficult to find appropriate educational services, and it may often be the lack of a good educational fit that contributes to the difficulties some highly gifted children encounter. This is part of Maureen Neihart's three-factor model – giftedness does influence psychological outcomes, but whether those outcomes are positive or negative depends on a complex interaction of the degree of giftedness, educational fit and individual characteristics.[116]

Social anxiety

Social anxiety disorder is a specific type of anxiety that gets triggered when children or adults are asked to think about or take part in social situations. It is more than shyness – it's an intense fear that makes it hard to build friendships and enjoy other people's company.[118] For example, Luka said that he was *"initially introverted, not socially skilled naturally – I had to tell myself to look people in the eye."* Children with social anxiety disorder worry about making social mistakes and may avoid going to places where they could learn social rules and how to act around others.

Learning and thinking differences can play a big role in social anxiety. Pupils with such differences can struggle with unstructured social interaction. They may get confused by the words people are using, or misread body language and other subtle cues. **Maria** says this has hampered interpersonal relationships throughout her life. **Dylan** needs to control: *"He gets very anxious about the routine of the school day, wants to know what's happening within each subject"*, says his teacher. Dylan has been isolated by classmates

---

117 www.studyandcareers.ie/online-courses
118 Schultz, J. (2022) *Social Anxiety in Kids: What You Need to Know*. Understood [online].

for *"persistently correcting others"*, but he is learning the hard way: *"I have been left out as a result of being over-honest. It's been hard… there's a point when honesty is going too far – just keep your mouth shut!"*

Anxiety and twice-exceptional learners

Gifted learners with co-existing learning challenges can be particularly vulnerable to anxiety. For example, anxiety is up to three times more common in children who are diagnosed with ADHD than in those who are not. A child with ADHD may blurt out something inappropriate, and a negative reaction from classmates may lead him or her to start avoiding group conversations. Similarly, a dyslexic child may avoid reading aloud in class by asking to go to the toilet, and this separation can reinforce the fear of reading aloud. The longer children with reading issues go without effective interventions, the more likely they are to develop social anxiety.

Whenever anxious gifted students are in a situation where they don't believe they will be successful, their brain instinctively interprets this as a threat to run away from. Their executive functioning skills take a back seat to fear, and the reasoning part of their brain becomes less efficient. Some anxious gifted learners find that meditation and mindfulness techniques can be useful in moderating feelings of worry and anxiety; **Luka** said it helps him to counteract over-thinking by *"feeling my living presence, not just my thoughts all the time."*

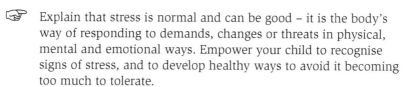 **How to help – stress and anxiety**

Strategies for parents and caregivers:

☞ Explain that stress is normal and can be good – it is the body's way of responding to demands, changes or threats in physical, mental and emotional ways. Empower your child to recognise signs of stress, and to develop healthy ways to avoid it becoming too much to tolerate.

☞ Encourage your child to 'befriend' their anxiety. Anxiety is not easy to bear, but resisting it can make things worse. Help them learn to accept it, like an old friend, and to reassure themselves that they will be fine. This is the ARC approach – accept, release, offer compassion.

☞ Source good children's books on the topics you need help with. For example, I have discussed death and bereavement using the book *Granpa*.[119] The cover image of an empty chair was powerful.

☞ Teach self-care skills – practising self-affirmation, taking personal responsibility for responding to stress, and understanding yourself and your goals. If worry begins to become unmanageable, seek help.

☞ Build grounding practices into your child's daily life. Mindfulness is one way to do this; the Alexander Technique is another. There is a wealth of online material to help with both (and see below).

Strategies for teachers and schools:

☞ Teach the power of the breath. Deep-belly breathing can alter parts of the brain tied to emotion and attention. Put your hands on your belly, inhale so your belly rises, hold for five seconds and exhale with a whispered 'R'. Doing this five times grounds and relaxes you.

☞ Mindfulness is a development of breathwork. Resources like *The Gifted Kids Workbook* provide a useful mix of mindfulness, Acceptance and Commitment Therapy (ACT), and self-compassion strategies.[120]

☞ The PSHE (personal, social and health education) curriculum is often critical for gifted learners. Topics such as feelings, friendships, group work, decision-making and bullying may present challenges for them and are important to address.

☞ Teach emotional literacy. This helps to pinpoint a learner's strengths, challenges and difficulties by measuring their ability to understand and express feelings, highlighting areas for intervention.[121]

☞ Use creative outlets to explore gifted learners' feelings and holistic development – for example artwork, vision-boards, singing, dancing and exercise. These activities lower stress levels and make school fun.

---

119 Burningham, J. (2003) *Granpa*. Red Fox

120 Boorman, H. & Kottmeyer, C. (2018) *The Gifted Kids Workbook: Mindfulness Skills to Help Children Reduce Stress, Balance Emotions, and Build Confidence*. New Harbinger.

121 Faupel, A. (2003) *Emotional literacy: Assessment and intervention: ages 11 to 16. User's guide*. GL Assessment.

Part 6: Inclusion and curriculum provision

Chapter 21: Underachieving gifted learners

Underachievement in gifted learners is a complex phenomenon, and it can be a major cause for concern among parents, teachers and indeed gifted students themselves. It occurs for a range of reasons, with boys twice as susceptible as girls. If we are to help these students, we need to explore the possible causes of their underachievement. This is far from simple – gifted learners are a diverse population with differing profiles, and their talents and strengths vary as widely as within any group of young people.

> ### Expert View
>
> *"One of the most intriguing and often frustrating puzzles is why some bright students never reach the level of success of which they seem so capable."*[75]
>
> Pamela Clinkenbeard

When we think about gifted learners, we tend to think of them as high-achieving, highly motivated individuals. But at times, many of our gifted students experience a discrepancy between ability and achievement – meaning that indicators such as intelligence assessments show that they possess high ability, but their school assessments do not. Essentially, their performance falls below what is expected based on their measured ability. While the insightful educator will know that assessment of a child's ability shouldn't rely on a test score only, it is nevertheless vital that we recognise signs of underachievement and have strategies in place to try to reverse it.

Researchers have settled on the following three criteria as representing broad agreement as to what constitutes underachievement:

1. A discrepancy between ability and achievement.
2. Performing below perceived ability must have persisted for at least a year.
3. There is no physical, mental or learning disability at the time.

This definition is a useful starting point; however, it is very basic and does not convey the complexity and diversity of gifted learners.[122] This author would be concerned about the requirement for 'performing below perceived ability to persist for at least a year' – this seems a long time to

---

[122] Post, G. (2016) *Who is the gifted underachiever? Four types of underachievement in gifted children.* Gifted Challenges [online].

allow underachievement to develop into a pattern and become embedded, if indeed that's what it is.

Types of gifted underachiever

Being able to recognise different types of gifted underachievers is crucial for effective intervention. When gifted students start displaying key signs, it's time to establish the root cause and seek appropriate support. Gail Post lists four different types of gifted underachiever to be aware of:[123]

1. Involuntary underachievers

These are students who would like to succeed, but their underachievement is caused by an absence of educational options – it does not result from personal, family or peer conflicts. A number of the gifted learners interviewed fell into this category, meaning they would have been better served if they had had a more personalised programme available to them.

2. Classic underachievers

These underachievers underperform in all areas of study. They have given up on school and themselves. Signs of boredom or depression may manifest in primary school. They are often angry, apathetic, rebellious or withdrawn.

3. Selective underachievers

These underachievers are active consumers – they seem to excel only in areas that interest them or within classes where they like or respect their teacher. Otherwise, they exert little effort, although they are perfectly capable of doing so. Their unwillingness to achieve in other classes limits their academic development, can set an unhealthy precedent for future learning and may affect their opportunities beyond school. **Luka** is perhaps an example of a selective underachiever – his interests in Music and French outshone all else, and ultimately these were the areas in which he achieved his degree.

4. Under-the-radar underachievers

These are the exceptionally gifted students who coast through school, often receiving average to high grades, but fail to reach their potential. Given their performance, their lack of effort often goes unrecognised and they are rarely encouraged to challenge themselves. Consequently, they may never learn how to take academic risks, experience and learn from failure, or develop resilience. These life lessons often occur much later – in college or at work – where they may feel blindsided because of lack of preparation.

Maria's experiences are mirrored in this description.

Causes of underachievement

Underachievement in gifted students can result from a variety of causes, including social issues, emotional sensitivities, an unchallenging curriculum, undiagnosed learning disabilities, and unsupportive home and school environments. Establishing the root causes of underachievement is not easy. Is the underachievement due to inappropriate teaching, learning and curriculum, an undiagnosed learning disability, poverty or disadvantaged environments, lack of teacher skill or social pressure? Or is it psychological?

Parents and educators must explore the causes of underachievement if they are to help these learners. Once a cause is identified, it's easier to address. Until then it's like shooting in the dark, and an inappropriate intervention can be harmful.[123] Scholars have argued that underachievement on the part of bright students occurs for one of three basic reasons:[124]

1. An apparent underachievement problem masks more serious physical, cognitive, or emotional issues.
2. The underachievement is symptomatic of a mismatch between the student and his or her school environment.[125]
3. Underachievement results from a personal characteristic such as low self-motivation, low self-regulation, or low self-efficacy.

Within the classroom, underachievement may manifest in a number of ways. In **Dylan**'s case (below) his mother describes the complexity of her twelve-year-old son's underachievement. It shows that Dylan has, in essence, aspects of all three reasons highlighted above. Potential causes, signs and interventions are hinted at in the underlines, and the table that follows shows a range of potential responses to Dylan's issues.

> "Teachers have to see past <u>how slowly he completes a task</u> to see that he can produce something good. But the <u>teacher</u> has to be willing to see that. He is also <u>prone to anxiety</u>, he is so sensitive. This totally messes with his ability to work. He still doesn't believe he is gifted as he sees others in class flying through work and because he doesn't, he feels less than them… so it reinforces the <u>feeling that he is less</u>. He doesn't place value on how original the stuff he comes up with is. Maybe in a task at school <u>where originality rather than speed is needed, he might feel more valued</u>. And, of course, <u>perfectionism</u> is a big problem.

---

123 Eide, B.L. & Eide, F.F. (2006) The Mislabeled Child. *The New Atlantis* [online].
124 Reis, S.M. & McCoach, D.B. (2000) The underachievement of gifted students: What do we know and where do we go? *Gifted Child Quarterly*, 44, 152-170.
125 McCoach, D.B. & Siegle, D. (2003) Factors That Differentiate Underachieving Gifted Students From High-Achieving Gifted Students. *Gifted Child Quarterly*, 47(2), 144-154.

> For example, the assignment is to put two words in a sentence. The others may write any old thing – whereas his sentences are often very fancy and funny, but it takes him ages. That said, his motivation matters – if he was doing homework at a friend's house and he got to play sooner by doing it faster he would... but left to his own devices he would be at it for an age. At the gifted learner course, he loved it because in that scenario being clever, putting the hand up, being heard was acceptable, not annoying to others."

Potential responses to Dylan's case

Causes and signs of underachievement	Potential interventions and ways forward
1. Teacher doesn't understand student.	CPD should be available to enable teacher to learn more about giftedness and inclusive classrooms, and differentiate approaches accordingly.
2. Student is prone to anxiety.	Student benefits from one-to-one discussions on feelings and sensitivities/over-excitabilities, and keeps a diary of feelings and originating thoughts/events for later discussion. Teacher assures student of personal support, keeps in contact with home and may make a referral, if there is no improvement.
3. Student feels he is less than the others.	Teacher builds a supportive classroom and implements PSHE programme, focusing on accepting difference, feelings and emotional literacy (GL assessment). Teacher uses flexible groupings to provide individual and small group feedback support that the student thrives on.
4. Student is slow to do his work and can be perfectionist.	Teacher and student discuss expectations around work responsibilities and deadlines. Teacher explains the signs and risks of perfectionism and encourages student to be metacognitive so he recognises when he may be paralysed by or procrastinating as a result of perfectionism. Teacher gives him autonomy and allows time flexibility for quality work produced.
5. Student isn't always motivated.	Teacher tests a range of approaches to see when the student is more motivated. Deadlines and rewards may help initially, especially rewards related to his interests. In an effort to understand student, teacher asks what motivates him and when he finds it easier to be motivated. Ultimately, the teacher wants to discover what intrinsically motivates the student so he will take ownership for his work.

How to help – underachievement

Strategies for parents and caregivers:

☞ Collaborate with the school. Parents and teachers are both holders of information vital to a learner's overall wellbeing. Underachievement is often identified at school, but parents can also share areas that their child identifies as problems in class. Together, parents and teachers can create supporting pathways for reversing underachievement.

☞ Talk up school and teachers in the home (for example, "nobody likes every teacher", "we all need to take personal responsibility"). This may be vital to dispel any misconceptions or negativity the underachieving gifted learner may feel towards school and teachers.

☞ Seek counselling if appropriate. Gifted learners may benefit from a specific safe space that allows them to share and deconstruct emotional and social obstacles that may impede achievement.

☞ Be an advocate for your child. Show that you believe in them and expect them to achieve. Bridge the gap between ability and achievement and nurture their gifts in ways that empower their future.

Strategies for teachers and schools:

☞ Identify the root causes. Once a cause is identified, you're on your way and can implement appropriate responses to effect increased drive, excitement and internal motivation towards achievement.

☞ Intervene early. The longer a child underachieves, the harder it is to reverse. Offer intervention for your gifted student as soon as you see their need. Don't wait until it's too late – you may lose them. Advanced material can be provided as early as the age of seven.[126]

☞ Engage mentors or volunteer teachers that gifted students respect, and who use time before and/or after school to work on activities. They can have long-lasting positive impacts on gifted underachievers.

---

126 Bainbridge, C. (2021) *Underachievement in Gifted Children*. Verywell Family [online].

Differentiate with a personal programme. Key considerations include:

- Find out what motivates the student to start achieving. Ask yourself – does the learning environment really provide an opportunity for them to explore their interests or passions?
- Gather information by talking with them, for example using a Proust-style interview.
- Offer academic choices from a menu of cognitively complex tasks.
- Challenge them. Gifted children who aren't challenged with a differentiated curriculum may 'give up' caring about learning or schoolwork, whereas work that is intellectually challenging is likely to motivate an intrinsically-motivated underachiever.[75]
- Connect students to high-achieving peers in the classroom or wider school. Encourage their collaboration. Be aware that due to social difficulties they may need an introduction!
- Connect conversations about the impact of school to future goals and learning, with reference to dreams, personal plans, further education and careers.
- Correct misconceptions – for example, the gifted learner may not view effort or task-commitment as being part of intelligence. This is an important one to address.
- Watch the impact of peers and social pressure on motivation. Gifted learners often hide their light for fear of being teased.

Chapter 22: The twice-exceptional (2e) learner

For some gifted learners, underachievement occurs as a result of co-existing special needs. Such needs may include a wide range of conditions including learning and/or emotional problems. These gifted learners are referred to as 'twice-exceptional' learners. 'Twice exceptional' (2e) is a term used to describe learners who are gifted and also have a specific learning difficulty; approximately one in six gifted learners falls into this category.[17] Twice-exceptional learners are more likely to experience underachievement because often efforts to address their needs may focus more on the remediation of difficulties than on the development of their strengths and talents.[125] Furthermore, programming for these learners can be difficult because their abilities often straddle both ends of the bell curve, with strengths and weaknesses needing to be simultaneously addressed in order for interventions to be successful.[127]

> ## Expert View
>
> "Too often the strengths of gifted disabled learners are unrecognised, ignored, or irksome because they are the wrong talents for conventional school achievement."[128]
>
> Susan Baum and Steven Owen

Research indicates that many 'twice-exceptional' students underachieve in school. A study of high-ability students with learning difficulties who were successful in higher education found that many of them had experienced periods of underachievement in primary and/or secondary education.[129] A problem that may arise is understanding the difference between gifted learners with motivation issues, and those with a specific learning difficulty. Some gifted learners may even underachieve deliberately in order to fit in. **Luka**'s underachievement is not due to a learning difficulty; rather, it is due to his inner struggle to cope with giftedness.

---

127 Schuler, P., Amend, E.R., Beaver-Gavin, K. & Beights, R. (2009) A Unique Challenge: Sorting Out the Differences between Giftedness and Asperger's Disorder. *Gifted Child Today*, 32(4), 57-63.

128 Baum, S. & Owen, S.V. (1988) High Ability/Learning Disabled Students: How Are They Different? *Gifted Child Quarterly*, 32(3), 321-326.

129 Reis, S.M., Neu, T.W. & McGuire, J.M. (1997). Case studies of high-ability students with learning disabilities who have achieved. *Exceptional Children*, 63(4), 463-479.

> "I had a slight fear of being classified as nerdy – felt insecure when confronted with things I found difficult or things I didn't excel in – and I let that affect my overall confidence in my ability. Maybe a lack of general opportunity at a young age to showcase more niche abilities (I always wanted to do a spelling bee, for example). In secondary school, I was more concerned with social ability than academic. It wasn't until final year in university when I cut down on partying and started actually going to the library and working on my thesis, that I remembered I was very good at academia and writing."

This chapter explores some of the difficulties that gifted learners may present with and suggests ways to respond. An important consideration for teachers to be aware of when teaching twice-exceptional learners is to be careful not to perpetuate their experience of underachievement by focusing more on remediation of their difficulties than development of their strengths and talents. When we give them opportunities to shine, twice exceptional learners are likely to find ways to compensate for their difficulties. I have seen this work to great effect for student and teacher.

Hearing difficulties

Children with hearing impairments exhibit similar characteristics of giftedness to hearing peers (eagerness to learn, visual skills, superior powers of recall, quick understanding, superior reasoning ability, or expressive language) except for their academic achievement, which could be delayed by up to four or five years. Hearing impairments should be ruled out as a first step when assessing underachieving gifted learners.

Specific learning difficulties

Research on gifted students with specific learning difficulties (such as dyslexia, dyscalculia, dysgraphia and Developmental Coordination Disorder) is challenging because of problems in defining each population, but it is certain that high ability students with such difficulties often underachieve.[125] Gifted students with specific learning difficulties may display high levels of creative potential, along with a tendency to behave disruptively and to achieve low levels of academic success, resulting in underachievement.[147] Dr Susan Baum, Director of the National Institute for 2e Research and Development at Bridges Academy in Los Angeles, identified four how-to-help strategies for gifted students with specific learning difficulties:[130]

---

130 Baum, S.M. (1994). Meeting the Needs of Gifted/Learning Disabled Students: How Far Have We Come? *Journal of Secondary Gifted Education*, 5(3), 6-22.

- encourage compensation strategies
- promote awareness of strengths and weaknesses
- focus on developing the child's gift
- provide an environment that values individual differences

Understandably, students who exhibit characteristics of giftedness and learning difficulty pose dilemmas for educators. The misconceptions, definitions, and expected outcomes for these types of students further complicate the issues facing appropriate programming for this population. In 1997, Sally Reis, Terry Neu and Joan Maguire compiled positive and negative characteristics of twice exceptional students. The outcome of this work is reproduced below.[130] The negative characteristics, which often result from the interaction of the student's high abilities and their learning difficulties, may hamper students' identification as gifted.

Table 22.1: Characteristics of Twice-Exceptional Students (adapted from Reid et al. (1997)

Gifted characteristics	Characteristics hampering identification as gifted
- Advanced vocabulary use - Exceptional analytic abilities - High levels of creativity - Advanced problem-solving skills - Ability to think of divergent ideas and solutions - Specific aptitude (artistic, musical, or mechanical) - Wide variety of interests - Good memory - Task commitment - Spatial abilities	- Frustration with inability to master certain academic skills (e.g. writing) - Learned helplessness - General lack of motivation - Disruptive classroom behaviour - Perfectionism - Super-sensitivity - Failure to complete assignments - Lack of organisational skills - Demonstration of poor listening and concentration skills - Deficiency in tasks emphasising memory and perceptual abilities - Low self-esteem - Unrealistic self-expectations - Absence of social skills with peers

ADHD

Giftedness and ADHD (Attention Deficit Hyperactivity Disorder) may co-occur. Complicating matters further, gifted students and those with ADHD may exhibit some similar behaviours – for example inattention, high levels of energy and impulsivity. Significantly, though, to distinguish whether a gifted student may also have ADHD, the school and home situation must be closely monitored because gifted children typically will not display similar behaviours in all settings (for example they may be attentive and successful in a music lesson but not in class), whereas children with ADHD will exhibit disordered behaviour in most or all environments.[125]

Emotional and behavioural problems

Gifted learners with emotional and behavioural problems are a particularly fraught cohort who are at risk of poor outcomes unless a holistic approach is adopted early by all stakeholders. Studies have found that these young people often experience periods of underachievement as a result of their disorders, that they are often under-challenged in school, escalating their problems, and that many drop out of school and are not recommended for gifted programmes.[131] Often the period that causes the most difficulty for these students is classroom 'dead time' – the period when they are awaiting instructions to challenge them while classmates finish their work.

Psychological issues

While the prevalence of psychological disorders is broadly similar within the gifted and non-gifted populations, it is important to be aware that many serious psychological illnesses such as schizophrenia and bipolar disorder generally have their onset in early to late adolescence.[132] Understandably, students who experience episodes of acute psychological distress or a more prolonged psychological condition may experience sudden and severe periods of academic underachievement.[125]

Grief and depression

Just like any other young people, gifted students can suffer grief and it can have a significant impact on their academic performance. The loss of a family member or a much-loved pet, as well as wider family problems like divorce or moving home, can cause them to experience stress, grief and anxiety. Gifted children can also be more prone than their peers to existential depression. This can cause them to question the

---

131 Reid, B.D. & McGuire, M.D. (1995). *Square pegs in round holes – These kids don't fit: High ability students with behavioral problems*. National Research Center on the Gifted and Talented.

132 McCrady, B.S. & Ziedonis, D. (2001) American Psychiatric Association practice guideline for substance use disorders. *Behavior Therapy*, 32(2), 309-336.

meaning of life and, in its most severe form, to reach the conclusion that life is meaningless.[142]

Bullying

Bullying may also cause depression. Some gifted learners may be targeted because others are envious of their abilities or the attention they receive, or because they're simply seen as 'different'. **Lucy**'s mother dealt expertly with the 'attention issue' within her family by explaining to her two older daughters the way Lucy saw, felt and understood the world. By doing so, she developed empathy and understanding in Lucy's older siblings.

Autism Spectrum Disorder (ASD)

Some gifted children may have Autism Spectrum Disorder (ASD) – especially in its mild (Level 1) form, which was until recently also known as Asperger's Disorder. Autism Spectrum Disorder is characterised by severe deficits in age-appropriate social interactions and restricted, repetitive patterns of behaviour or interests. This combination can have a profound impact on both social interactions and schooling.[133]

Difficulties can arise because some characteristics of giftedness are also seen in students with autism. Although superficially similar, the behaviours may present differently and/or the motivation for them may be different.[134] Appendix 5 contains a very useful checklist for assessing the psychological and educational needs of a student, indicating which interventions may be most appropriate and deciding whether to refer them for formal evaluation.

Cerebral palsy (CP)

Children with cerebral palsy (CP) can also be gifted. Cerebral palsy is a group of disorders that affect a person's ability to move and maintain balance and posture.[135] It may also affect speech. When faced with an extreme disability such as cerebral palsy, teachers may be in danger of focusing on the students' areas of weakness only rather than their areas of strength. It is important that we enable seriously disabled students to have the opportunity to show us their strengths and intellectual abilities.

---

133 Amend, E.R., Schuler, P., Beaver-Gavin, K. & Beights, R. (2009) A Unique Challenge: Sorting Out the Differences between Giftedness and Asperger's Disorder. *Gifted Child Today*, 32(4), 57-63.
134 David, H. (2019). Learning Disabilities, Attention Deficit (Hyperactivity) Disorder, and Intelligence. *Davidson Institute*, 13.
135 CDC (2022) *What is Cerebral Palsy?* Centers for Disease Control and Prevention.

How to help – the twice-exceptional learner

☞ Formulate a profile of the learner's interests, talents and abilities. This can be done at any time, but it is particularly useful at the start of the year so the teacher has a full picture from the outset.

☞ Observe students and note where they excel and struggle. Keep samples of their work and note patterns that emerge to discuss with the learner, parents, other teachers and psychologists.

☞ Recognise the difference between academic motivation issues and a gifted learner with a learning difficulty. Study carefully the internal scores of intelligence tests and standardised test results, not just the cumulative scores, to get a more precise picture of where the student's strengths and weaknesses lie.

☞ If a learner displays uneven skills, conduct a thorough pre-referral intervention phase, adjusting environment and curriculum in order to focus on strengths and accommodate weaknesses. Respond to findings with a suitably differentiated curriculum and environment. Involve the learner and parents in formulating an Individual Education Plan (IEP) with agreed actions and targets.

☞ Be aware of signs of psychological distress and alert to bullying, grief and depression. Discuss with parents and respond with a supportive, listening ear. Research local groups that may be able to offer support. Conduct a pre-referral intervention to establish a full picture and refer learner to a counsellor, psychologist or doctor for help if necessary.

☞ If the learner displays behavioural issues, keep a log of observations and seek a qualified professional to consider whether the difficulties may stem from giftedness or from other causes such as ADHD.

☞ If autism is suspected, use the checklist in Appendix 5 to distinguish between a gifted learner and a student with ASD. If most ticks are in the gifted column, implement curriculum modification and differentiation. If most are on the autism side or the split is fairly even, deploy strategies to address the specific behaviours observed and seek appropriate professional support.

☞ Teachers should seek and be provided with specific training and upskilling in this complex area. They can only look past a learning difficulty and recognise a child's potential if they are aware of it.

Chapter 23: Curriculum differentiation

Gifted learners are a diverse group – their characteristics and needs are personal and unique. They vary in abilities and aptitudes, and they may demonstrate gifts and talents either in a single domain or across a range of areas. They may also have a disability and/or specific learning difficulty. In short, they differ from the bright, convergent thinkers for whom education systems are primarily designed. So how do we support an 'at-risk' population that most people don't recognise as being at-risk, and which in fact most people see as 'lucky' and therefore not requiring support?

> *Expert View*
>
> *"Gifted learners need an appropriately differentiated curriculum designed to address their individual characteristics, needs, abilities, and interests."*
>
> Sandra Berger

Gifted learners need time for in-depth exploration, manipulating ideas and drawing generalisations about seemingly unconnected concepts, and they ask provocative questions.[136] If they are to one day realise the potential of their gift, they need the opportunity to make continuous learning progress in school – which means they need curricula, instruction and assessment that are differentiated in level, complexity, depth and pacing in line with their requirements.[137] Regular curriculum review is essential to ensure the fulfilment of their need for increasingly complex and challenging tasks.

All models of giftedness, as we saw in Part 1, view giftedness as a broad concept covering a range of abilities.[138] They recognise that exceptional ability needs to undergo some transformational process if it is to be reflected in high levels of achievement or talent, and that school plays a critical role in giving gifted students the opportunities, stimulation and experiences to develop their potential and translate their gifts into talents.

There is no 'one size fits all' approach – the best programme for a gifted learner is one that meets their needs wherever they currently are and plans from that point forward, in collaboration. Ironically, in

---

136 Berger, S.L. (1991) *Differentiating curriculum for gifted students*. Davidson Institute [online].
137 Rogers, K.B. (2002) *Re-forming Gifted Education: Matching the Program to the Child*. Great Potential Press.
138 TCEO (2008) *Student Diversity*. Tasmanian Catholic Education Office [online].

the COVID-19 environment, the prevalence of online learning – an asynchronous model that allows each student to progress at his or her own pace – was an approach that suited many gifted learners.

Developing curricula that are sufficiently rigorous, challenging and coherent for gifted students is not easy. The goal is for an appropriately differentiated curriculum to produce well-educated, knowledgeable students who have worked hard, mastered a substantial body of knowledge, and can think clearly and critically about that knowledge. This process produces high levels of satisfaction for students and teachers.[159] Curricula should give also due regard to socio-emotional as well as cognitive development, and leadership education should be incorporated. [95]

What is an effective curriculum?

In her synthesis of curriculum effectiveness studies and effective practice, Sandra Berger suggests that a differentiated curriculum would respond to the diverse characteristics of gifted learners in the following three ways:[159]

1. Accelerating mastery of basic skills through testing-out procedures and reorganising the curriculum according to higher level skills and concepts.
2. Engaging students in active problem-finding and problem-solving activities and research.
3. Providing students with opportunities for making connections within and across systems of knowledge by focusing on issues, themes and ideas.

Gifted learners also need an appropriately differentiated curriculum designed to address their individual needs, with regular opportunities to work and be challenged in their areas of interest, passion and talent. It is vital too that gifted learners be given access to instructional resources and activities that are commensurate with their talents, as it is only through this that they will make significant progress.[139]

So an effective curriculum for gifted students is essentially a basic curriculum modified to meet their needs. Their unique characteristics should serve as the basis for decisions on how it should be modified. A programme that builds on these characteristics may be viewed as qualitatively (rather than quantitatively) different from a basic curriculum; it results from appropriate modification of content, process, environment and product.[140]

---

139 Bate, J., Clark, D. & Riley, T. (2012) Gifted Kids Curriculum: What Do the Students Say? *Kairaranga*, 13(2) 23-28.
140 Maker, C.J. & Nielson, A.B. (1996) *Curriculum Development and Teaching Strategies for Gifted Learners*. 2nd ed. PRO-ED.

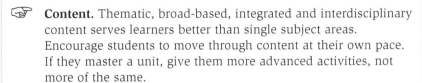
How to help – curriculum modification

The following four major factors should be considered when modifying curricula to meet the needs of gifted learners:

- **Content.** Thematic, broad-based, integrated and interdisciplinary content serves learners better than single subject areas. Encourage students to move through content at their own pace. If they master a unit, give them more advanced activities, not more of the same.

- **Process.** To modify process, activities must be restructured to be more intellectually demanding. Give students open-ended questions, stimulate higher-level thinking skills, and encourage them to think about subjects in more complex, abstract and exploratory ways.

- **Environment.** Gifted students learn best in a non-judgemental climate that fosters curiosity and connects school to the outside world. Establish an environment that encourages them to question, exercise independence and use creativity to be all they can be.

- **Product.** Learners should be encouraged to use a range of forms to show their knowledge and ability to manipulate ideas. Ask them to address real-world issues and to synthesise rather than summarise. Vary assessment approaches, and allow consistency with each student's preferred learning style.

Universal Design for Learning (UDL)

First defined by Dr David Rose of the Center for Applied Special Technology (CAST) and the Harvard Graduate School of Education, Universal Design for Learning (UDL) is a set of principles, a framework and a field that guides teachers in developing instructional goals, environments, assessments, methods and materials to meet the diverse needs of all learners.

UDL approaches can fulfil the requirements of an effective differentiated curriculum by allowing gifted learners to pursue areas of passion and interest, and to research their own topics by creating their own questions that they want to find answers to. The curriculum can be integrated across different subject areas to support the connective thinking inherent in divergence, and a strengths-based approach can allow gifted learners to appreciate their own areas of talent while also recognising the gifts and talents of others – so vital for developing understanding and empathy.

The Three Block Model of UDL

Dr Jennifer Katz of the University of British Columbia created the Three Block Model of UDL, which is designed to make the social and academic life of the classroom accessible for all students. The Three Block Model recognises that learners require supports for social and emotional learning, as well as intellectual engagement, growth and success.

According to Katz, the Three Block Model, where implemented across primary and secondary schools, has been shown to increase academic achievement, student engagement, self-concept, respect for diverse others, prosocial behaviour, and teacher satisfaction and self-efficacy.

Several strategies built into the Three Block Model support the inclusion of students who are gifted, and it should be strongly considered as a useful tool by educators.[13]

Systems and Structures	Inclusive Instructional Practice

■ Inclusive Policy – No "Except!"
■ Visionary, instructional leadership
■ Distributed leadership
■ In-depth professional development
■ Staffing for collaborative practice
   ■ Team planning time
   ■ Scheduling in cohorts/teams
   ■ Resource/EA allocations to classrooms
   ■ Co-planning/teaching/assessing
■ Budgeting changed from segregated practices/funding allocations
   ■ Assistive technology available to all
   ■ Multi-leveled resources
■ School and district culture of care and inclusivity
■ Curriculum designed for diversity
■ Flexible learning environment
	■ Integrated Curriculum – Cross-Curricular Connections
	■ Student Choice and Autonomy
	■ Flexible Groupings/Cooperative Learning
	■ Differentiated Instruction and Assessment
	■ Self-Regulated Learning
	■ Assessment for Learning/Class Profiles
	■ Technology
	■ Discipline-Based Inquiry
	■ Meta-Cognition
	■ Understanding by Design
	■ Problem-Based Learning
	■ Inquiry
	■ Social & Academic Inclusion as Guiding Principle for Tier 2/3 supports

Social and Emotional Learning and Well-Being: Developing Compassionate Classroom Communities

- Developing Self-Concept
  - Awareness of and pride in strengths and challenges
- Sense of Belonging
- Self-Regulation
  - Goal setting and planning
  - Emotional regulation, mindfulness
- Valuing Diversity
  - Awareness of the strengths and challenges of others
  - Valuing of diverse contributions to community
  - Sense of collective responsibility for well-being, achievement of all
  - Empathy, perspective taking, compassion
- Democratic Classroom Management
  - Collective problem solving, recognition of rights and responsibilities
  - Promotion of independent learning, student choice and empowerment, leadership
- Positive Mental Health for Teachers and Students
- Resiliency and Distress Tolerance
- Indigenous Perspectives on Health, Healing, and Reconciliation
- Service Education – developing meaning and purpose
- Programming
  - Respecting Diversity Program (RD), Spirity Buddies, Class Meetings, Brain Unit, DBT, Mindfulness
  - TRC programming

Figure 23.1: The Three Block Model of UDL (Katz)

How to help – a differentiated curriculum

☞ Effective differentiation for gifted students consists of carefully planned, coordinated learning experiences that extend the core curriculum, combine enrichment and acceleration strategies and engage learners at appropriate levels of challenge.

☞ Parents and teachers should ensure that gifted children have access to a selection of advanced supplementary reading materials in their topic of choice. Also allow them to suggest extra resources that may be useful for the school or class library.

☞ Vary the method of presentation – small/large groups, experiments, demonstration and lecture-style. It is important to avoid students copying notes when content is already mastered. Encourage them to present their learning in interesting ways for easier recall or sharing.

☞ Understanding by Design (UBD, also called Backwards Design) allows learners to focus on a holistic conceptual understanding of 'big ideas' such as racism and climate action. UBD considers assessments and goals before designing activities and is a good fit for gifted students.

☞ Class meetings, learning teams and use of the Respecting Diversity programme (or equivalent) assist students in developing a positive sense of self, and a sense of belonging within their school.[13]

☞ Counselling can be helpful. Teachers can use strategies such as bibliotherapy and video-therapy to allow students to explore strategies for social problem-solving and emotional coping.

Enrichment strategies offering more varied educational experiences, which build upon the regular curriculum and offer a deeper exploration of subject matter to challenge gifted learners include:

☞ Independent research: Students select and work on a topic of personal choice in which they show strength. Teacher agrees ground rules – for example, how much class time will be used, what the outcome will be and the form the end presentation will take. This is very useful for students who finish their required classwork early.

- ☞ Enrichment groups: Schedule a set time each week to bring together a small number of students with similar interests and abilities to pursue a topic of study, under the guidance of a teacher or mentor. Providing a resource class of this kind was a strong recommendation that emerged from my interviews with students and teachers.

- ☞ Learning contract: A teacher may agree a learning contract to keep a student working alongside peers most of the time while also allowing them choices about what and how to learn. It is important to have an agreed menu of choices to ensure the student uses their time wisely.

- ☞ Mentors: Connect your student's specialist knowledge area with a specialist in their field. A mentor may be another teacher, a volunteer parent or community member or another student. It may also take place online, under supervision.

- ☞ Interest centres: Allow the gifted student the freedom to create a centre in the classroom based on their specialist interest area, for sharing with and presentation to other pupils/classes.

- ☞ Assignments with increasing complexity are useful in skill areas where the student has not yet met the outcomes but requires additional challenge. For example, in English, the student may read more challenging texts, write in a more challenging genre (e.g. screenplay instead of narrative) or study more sophisticated vocabulary.

- ☞ More demanding assessment criteria: The assessment criteria for the assignment may be changed to suit the student's strengths – for example, a history report could become a PowerPoint, a Reader's Theatre or video presentation. The work will require at least five sources from the gifted student, but only three from the class.

- ☞ Extension work: Gifted learners are encouraged to complete the follow-up extension activities in textbooks when finished early. They may also practise setting their own assignment questions for their topic to reflect the learning they deem essential. Open-ended, real-world problems are excellent ways to extend gifted students' learning.

- ☞ Learning logs: Students keep logs of experiences they have outside the classroom that connect with their studies and increase their learning outcomes. They reflect on experiences that fulfilled them and say why. This provides useful insights for teachers and parents too.

> **Acceleration strategies** may also be useful in some cases:
>
> ☞ Skipping a class or grade – for example, where a student who is in third class or grade is promoted to fourth because they demonstrate the capability to handle that class level.
>
> ☞ Changing class level for a single subject only – a subject in which the gifted student shows extraordinary ability.
>
> ☞ Condensing the curriculum so that a gifted student gets several years of content in a single year. This requires considerable teacher skill, know-how and commitment.
>
> **NOTE:** Acceleration strategies come with a word of warning in relation to student suitability, particularly concerning their social and emotional development. Acceleration also requires agreement and timetabling with other class teacher(s) as well as considerable discussion with parent and gifted learner. Acceleration strategies are best tried on the basis of monitoring and regular review.

Chapter 24: Best practice to support gifted learners

Since I began writing this book, I've often been asked if there is an ideal teacher to support gifted learners. Experience has shown me that there are many ways to 'skin a cat' and it's rarely wise to be over-prescriptive. Gifted learners we know are a diverse group – but then so are teachers! That said, there are useful guiding principles that should inform best practice for teaching gifted learners. With effective, confident teachers that recognise and understand gifted learners and their needs, our students can thrive.

> *Key Point*
>
> *With effective, confident teachers that recognise and understand gifted learners and their needs, our students can thrive.*

What it takes to teach gifted learners well begins with the premise that every child should come to school each day to stretch and grow. There is the expectation that the main measure of progress is competition with oneself rather than with others. It also resides in the notion that educators understand the key concepts, principles and skills of their subject domains, and present them in ways that cause students to wonder, grasp and extend their reach. And it envisions schooling as an escalator on which students continually progress upwards and forward, rather than as a series of stairs, with landings on which advanced learners consistently wait.[141]

Easier said than done perhaps. When teachers follow a standardised approach rather than being flexible, reflective practitioners, it makes this very difficult to achieve. That said, in schools where responsive teaching and learning is a carefully supported indicator of professional growth, the ability to extend even the most capable mind becomes a benchmark of success. Studies appear to point to a need for assessment of teachers for both personality and professional qualifications before they are assigned to the gifted classroom, and for special courses to upskill teachers of gifted students. Openness to growth and learning as a teacher for this special cohort is essential.

---

[141] Tomlinson, C.A. (1997) *What it Means to Teach Gifted Learners Well.* National Association for Gifted Children.

Teacher skills and characteristics

A study conducted in 2016 in the Czech Republic investigated nearly one thousand teachers in lower-secondary education working with gifted pupils across different types of schools.[142] The results showed that the overall rate of teachers' self-assessment of their competence was slightly positive. Unsurprisingly perhaps, teachers with shorter practice, less experience and less training in the area of gifted pupils declared poorer self-assessment, whereas teachers with longer practice, more experience and education declared better self-assessment. Nevertheless, it was striking that almost half of teachers declared that they were not trained in the specific issue of giftedness at university or in further education. Similarly, in the studies conducted for this book, many of the teachers interviewed regretted their lack of foundational training and CPD in gifted education.

A separate Czech study undertaken in the same year examined the quality of differentiation of instruction with gifted pupils among six hundred teachers.[143] They found the teachers to be more able to differentiate curriculum than to differentiate didactic approaches in a mixed classroom and, interestingly, that women coped better with differentiation than men. Teachers working predominantly in humanities also coped better with differentiation than those working in the natural sciences.

In these studies, the personal characteristics of the teacher emerged as the most important influencing factor when working with gifted students. The teacher's understanding of and attitude towards the gifted learners matters most of all.[144] Students in an Israeli study concluded that teachers of gifted students ideally should have unique personal, intellectual and didactic characteristics and an attitude that empowers their students to realise their potential. Students placed more importance on the inherent personality of the teacher than on acquired teaching skills.[145]

In the interviews conducted for this book, the gifted learners were asked to select one teacher who 'got' them. In some cases they found this difficult. **Maria** felt no teacher ever understood her as a learner in the whole course of her education, and she nominated no teacher as a result.

---

[142] Kočvarová, I., Machů, E. & Petrujová, J. (2016) Self-assessment of teachers working with gifted pupils in terms of their work experience and education. In: *ICERI2016*: 9th

[143] Eva Machů, E., Kočvarová, I. & Kopřivovác, R. (2016) Tendencies of gifted pupils toward selected aspects of conformist behavior in the context of their relationships with classmates. *Procedia - Social and Behavioral Sciences* 217, 214-221.

[144] David, H. (2011) Teachers' Attitude: Its importance in nurturing and educating gifted children. *Gifted and Talented International*, 26(1-2), 65-80.

[145] Khalil, M. & Accariya, Z. (2016) Identifying "Good" Teachers for Gifted Students. *Creative Education*, 7, 407-418.

Miguel stressed the importance of a teacher's personal characteristics – in particular, their attitude and honesty in relation to teaching and learning.

Dos and don'ts for teaching gifted learners

Appropriate instruction for gifted learners should vary depending on each individual child's gender, culture, background and learning strengths. Understandably, there is a considerable difference between a child who comes to school rich with experiences versus a child who is equally able but lacks that richness of experience.[146] So there can be no 'one size fits all'.

Nonetheless, according to noted researchers such as Professor Carol Tomlinson of the University of Virginia and Dr Elissa Brown of the Hunter College Center for Gifted Education, there is broad agreement on a range of general indicators of appropriate and inappropriate instruction for gifted learners, with implications for teachers. Implementing the appropriate suggestions (dos) – and taking care to avoid the inappropriate ones (don'ts) – will set gifted learners on a trajectory towards developing their talents.

Dos

When gifted students are bored or unchallenged, it is a mismatch between the student's needs and the programme offered.[147] Teachers should learn about this special population, be committed to continuous professional development and seek out others with a vested interest in gifted learners. Teacher advocates are important in showing both learners and parents that a school understands and cares about the needs of gifted students.

Identify the specific areas in which each student is gifted. This can be done through formal and informal assessments so teachers can offer extension, enrichment, acceleration and complexity in that student's area of strength.

This may mean a different lesson plan, working with other teachers or finding additional resources.[173] Insipid curricula and instruction will not inspire gifted students. They need teachers who will provide them with rich learning experiences that are relevant to their lives, delivered in respectful environments that help them achieve more than they thought possible.[147]

Good teaching for gifted learners is paced in response to the student's individual needs. Often, gifted students learn more quickly than their

---

146 Tomlinson, C.A. (1997). The dos and don'ts of instruction: What it means to teach gifted learners well. *Instructional Leader*, 10(3), 1-3, 12.
147 Brown, E.F. (2015) Serving Gifted Students in General Ed Classrooms. *Edutopia* [online].

peers; however, it can also be the case that advanced learners need a slower pace of instruction so they can achieve the depth of understanding needed to satisfy a big appetite for knowledge.[147] Gifted students also need opportunities to work with intellectual peers in order to develop optimally.

Teaching the complex material that gifted learners need calls for more refined teacher skills. Content, processes and products should be more open-ended and multi-faceted than would be appropriate for many peers. Gifted learners should work with more abstract problems, will often need less teacher-imposed structure, and should have to make greater leaps of insight and transfer than would be appropriate for many young people of their age.[147] Critical thinking skills or creative activities should not be taught in isolation, but should be built on a solid foundation of high-level content.[173]

Good teaching for gifted learners requires an understanding of 'supported risk'. Generally, gifted learners succeed without regular encounters with failure. But, when a teacher presents a high-challenge task, the student may feel threatened. Not only is it unlikely that they have learned to study hard, take risks and strive, but the student's self-image may also be threatened. A good teacher of gifted students understands this dynamic, and is able to encourage and scaffold risk in a way that supports success.[147]

Don'ts

If there is a mismatch between classroom instruction and a gifted student's intellectual needs, then that may cause the pupil to 'act out' or misbehave. Gifted learners are developmentally asynchronous, meaning that their cognitive and emotional development are out of sync, so teachers should not expect children to be impeccably well-behaved just because they are gifted. Nor should they expect their gifted students to be gifted across every area – many have a gift in only one domain.[173]

Instruction for gifted learners is inappropriate when it asks them to do 'more of the same faster', or to repeat things that they have already mastered while others catch up. Instead, gifted learners should be pre-assessed and given an integrated, increasingly complex developmental programme – in other words, more advanced materials, ideas and skills when they demonstrate competency. Teachers should never 'fill time' by asking gifted learners to do a puzzle or classroom chores just because they've finished early.[147]

Gifted learners should not be separated from their class for long periods. Asking them to study alone ignores their need for meaningful teacher and peer interaction in the learning process, and it may negatively impact social and emotional development. Conversely, gifted learners should not spend extended time in the role of peer tutor. While this can be useful, students need to be colleagues for each other too, giving a hand or clarifying when needed.[147] That's very different from becoming a 'junior teacher' – a role that **Jess** frequently found herself in, and one that concerned her mother.

How to help – best practices for supporting gifted learning

Strategies for parents and caregivers:

- ☞ Recognise that gifted children are truly different and need advanced, intensive and accelerated instruction. Education, no matter how good, is likely to involve periods of downtime for them. As a parent you will need to supplement this in various ways to support their interests.

- ☞ Misunderstandings about giftedness are common. Those who haven't lived with, counselled or taught a gifted child may view them as odd, studious nerds who don't quite fit in, with parents running their lives. Eliminate these misconceptions wherever you find them.

- ☞ Agitate for legal provision. Adopting provisions in law gives families leverage to fight for their children's rights. Families frequently feel abandoned and rely on the school to help their son or daughter. No child should be denied their legal right to an appropriate education.

- ☞ Advocate for your child's rights – individually within the school, and through participation in parent groups, support for systemic change and public advocacy for policy change. Reform always takes time, so it's important to keep working with teachers to help your child adapt and prosper.

Strategies for teachers and schools:

- ☞ Find joy and uniqueness in each gifted child. Establish and maintain a warm and accepting classroom that understands their differences and similarities, maximise potential by expecting students to do their best, and remember that gifted children do not excel in all areas.

- ☞ Make the curriculum flexible and student-centred. Involve your gifted students in decision-making, giving them options and responsibility for their own learning. Encourage learning for its own sake, teach research skills and explore multiple points of view about contemporary topics.

- ☞ Teach interactively, with an emphasis on working together. Cluster gifted students where possible, and provide opportunities for gifted children to interact with other gifted children across grade levels and local schools through competitions and collaborative projects. Remember gifted students are 'idea mates' rather than 'age mates'.

- ☞ Provide opportunities for gifted children to engage in social activities and develop social skills – an area of difficulty for some. Address the counselling needs of gifted students as needed, keeping in mind that that about a quarter of gifted students have emotional difficulties.

- ☞ Ensure parental input in the education of gifted children. This may seem obvious, but given teacher time pressures it is easily overlooked. Encourage gifted students to participate in academic activities outside school such as maths clubs, chess clubs, writing groups, debating societies and quiz teams.

- ☞ Keep an open mind and research resources and approaches to suit your gifted learners. Consider the curriculum enrichment and acceleration strategies outlined in the previous chapter.

Part 7: Conclusion

Chapter 25: Summary

This chapter recaps on the main factors covered in this book that relate to the gifted learner and giftedness. I have indicated throughout why these factors are important. All gifted learners do not identify with or respond to each factor in the same way; hence it is crucial to have the specific gifted learner at the centre of your decision-making process and to personalise strategies to suit the needs, gifts and challenges of that individual.

Key Point

It is crucial to have the specific gifted learner at the centre of your decision-making process.

Asynchronous development

Gifted learners can be confusing and are not always easy to identify, largely because it is difficult to make generalisations about them as a group. It is impossible to say, for example: "All gifted learners are X". They are similar to and different from other learners in various ways. With that said, how gifted learners think and question does set them apart. Having conducted fifty-four interviews with and about gifted learners for this book, the single definition that I believe best captures their uniqueness is as follows:

> *"Giftedness is asynchronous development in which advanced cognitive abilities and heightened intensity combine to create inner experiences and awareness that are qualitatively different from the norm. This asynchrony increases with higher intellectual capacity. The uniqueness of the gifted renders them particularly vulnerable and requires modifications in parenting, teaching, and counselling in order for them to develop optimally."*[7]

'Asynchrony' is a term used to describe the mismatch that exists between a learner's cognitive, emotional and physical development. For example, a child may be excellent at reading, writing and language but weak in maths or vice versa. Or their intellectual or creative skills may be quite advanced, but their social and emotional development may be immature. For this reason, I agree with many professionals in the field that asynchronous development rather than potential or ability is the defining characteristic of giftedness.

Advanced learning characteristics

It was true of all the gifted learners interviewed that their teachers reported that they demonstrated the capacity to understand readily, learn quickly and easily and retain what is learned, particularly in their special interest areas. Gifted learners are typically avid readers with the ability to absorb books way beyond their years. Take note of their curiosity and problem-solving ability and let them show this – above all they need to be challenged, so don't hold back! Watch out for their ability to see subtle relationships and make connections within and across what may seem like unrelated topics, and give them the opportunity to justify their ideas. Their advanced intellectual development is evident in their superior reasoning powers, cognitive flexibility and ability to consider problems from different angles.

Curiosity and problem solving

The gifted learner who loves and thrives on maths is a problem-solver, whereas the scientific gifted learner tends to be more curious, asking persistent questions in order to solve problems and come up with solutions. The world needs these young innovative minds, so create an environment where they can explore and come up with new ideas. They need daily challenges. It is not enough to provide students with work to keep them busy or more of the same. Give them access to materials where they can progress at their own pace and incrementally improve level after level. This responds to their asynchronous developmental needs. Blended learning online programmes on topics of their choice are particularly appealing to them, and webinars are available on just about any topic that interests students. Gifted learners love the sense of accomplishment they get from material that challenges them at their level.

Creative ability

Gifted learners often demonstrate extraordinary creative talent. To continually develop, these students need outlets for their talent inside and outside the school in addition to ongoing tuition at their level. Because their intellectual and/or creative talent may be more advanced than their emotional development, they may be prone to anxiety. Anxiety craves reassurance – the gifted learner thrives on feedback and encouragement.

The provision of much extra-curricular support may depend on the parents' ability to provide for it financially and logistically. Schools need to be proactive in identifying and monitoring the gifted child or young person whose parents may not realise how talented their son or daughter is or have the means to support them. There may be bursaries or financial supports available for gifted learners from socially deprived backgrounds.

Sense of humour

There is a lot to deal with when it comes to gifted learners, so make use of humour. They can have a wicked sense of humour and see connections that may be lost on others! Conversely, they also need to know that they can benefit from adopting a light-hearted approach when they are taking themselves too seriously – it can ground them and help them let go of an issue. Light relief lets us breathe! And the great news is that laughter and worry do not co-exist in the nervous system, so capitalise on the humour.

Motivation and task commitment

A feature of gifted learners is their visible motivation and commitment to a task. They tend to show a strong awareness that school is linked to life purpose, unless they have become demotivated and are underachieving. This is what we want to guard against by ensuring appropriate learning challenges and opportunities are in place to meet the level of the learner. The 'task-committed' student shows outstanding responsibility and independence in classwork enabling them to sustain concentration for lengthy periods of time. TARGET (Tasks, Autonomy, Recognition, Grouping, Evaluation, Time) is a useful model to enable teachers to structure classroom practices to promote and support the student's motivation.

One of the most useful pieces of advice for parents and teachers is to nurture the gifted child's interests. A word of warning though – their interests can be intense, so go with the flow! Children who can explore their interests are more likely to keep their love of learning alive. Help your child too to make connections between schoolwork and their interests that may not be immediately apparent to them. And expose them to new ideas: sometimes learners lack motivation because they haven't yet been exposed to what might become a subject of interest or even a life passion.

Boredom

Many gifted learners experience boredom, so it is vital that teachers are prepared for it. In many respects it's easy to address boredom when teachers and parents cooperate and provide a menu of activities based on the learner's interests that they can choose from once classwork is completed. The need for teachers to recognise the valid input that parents can have and to seek the help of the parent to understand and meet their student's needs is critical. The mindset of the teacher is essential here so as not to be threatened or triggered by the word 'bored'. Encourage the child to figure out why they are bored and to come up with suggestions for more worthwhile experiences. Share the responsibility with them.

Competitiveness

The relationship that gifted learners have with competition and motivation is fascinating. The key determinant is how individuals orient themselves towards competition – are the students fuelled by the desire to improve their performance, or is it a drive to one-up someone else? Notice both types. Gifted learners are quite likely to need coaching through challenging situations such as working on group projects at school, handling winning and losing games, dealing with performance fears and coping with competition within families. Helping them to understand that winning and losing are temporary states, and that focusing solely on results can lead to disregarding others' feelings, can normalise anxiety and encourage a growth mindset.

Leadership

Leadership is a less recognised area of giftedness, but it is significant. Many gifted students carry responsibility well and have an ability to communicate with adults in a mature way. Leadership may manifest in those motivated by social justice, world problems and an interest in solving them. So, we must remember that motivation in a gifted learner may extend beyond school achievement. A gifted teenager who is motivated to create a community group for the elderly or help children with special needs is showing initiative and leadership, and this should be recognised and acknowledged.

Social and emotional development

Social and emotional development may be the most testing of all areas for the gifted student. As amazing, bright and demanding as they are, they are also fragile, vulnerable human beings who can struggle with self-acceptance. It is vital that parents and teachers build inclusive home environments and classrooms respectively, where children feel valued and know that their parents and teachers recognise and accept them for who they are – that they are 'good enough' in their own right and worthy of success.

Since the internal pressure that gifted learners place on themselves can in itself be debilitating, teachers and parents should collaborate to ensure there is no added external pressure making matters worse. Reinforcing that grades are important but not representative of the whole person helps learners understand that "grades don't make you a good person". Take note that the language of feelings can be very uncomfortable for gifted learners, and they are likely to need consistent support to apply it and believe it!

Perfectionism

Issues around perfectionism can also be barriers to learning and personal happiness for the gifted learner. Perfectionism is the relentless striving for high personal standards combined with overly critical self-evaluations, where a learner judges their own worth on their ability to achieve and where they persist despite huge personal cost. The problem arises because along the way, the affirmation they receive for great work has been mixed-up with the core of their self-esteem. Then, to maintain high standards/marks, they work even harder to meet their own expectations. In short, they are their own harshest critic. Some seek to cover this up; others don't!

Intensity and over-excitability

Perfectionism can also be coupled with intensity and over-excitability, where gifted learners react more strongly and for longer than normal to a stimulus that may be very small, affecting their central nervous system more intensely. Be aware of any sensitivities and accept the child's differences as part of who they are. Remind them that the body needs to be calm before the brain can work well. Provide sensory experiences to help with this, and be a calm and steady sounding board when things go wrong.

Worry and anxiety

It can be difficult to see past a learner's potential and glimpse the young person who may be anxious, lonely, confused or unsure of what the future might bring. For gifted students, these feelings and vulnerabilities associated with stress, social anxiety and exam worries are real despite their advanced development. As parents and educators, it is vital that we realise this even if we do not always immediately understand why. Our job is to support them through these times, enabling them to gain perspective and to learn coping strategies to help themselves. Watch for changing patterns of behaviour in teenagers and refer the child to a professional counsellor if appropriate – sometimes they are more comfortable opening up to someone else.

Provide a social network

There is unanimity across the literature regarding the importance of providing gifted learners with opportunities to engage with other gifted students. They can often feel isolated and lack a peer group in the mainstream classroom, so schools need to make an extra effort to get these students together at a whole school level, if only once a week. This is why gifted learners reportedly love having other people with whom they share similar interests, and find attending gifted learner groups extremely rewarding. Like all students, gifted students require a social network where they feel safe to share their unique interests, without fear of mockery.

Underachieving gifted learners

There are many reasons why gifted learners might underachieve. They may have been lost along the way in the education system – not recognised, understood, connected with or challenged. They may 'hide their light under a bushel' to fit in socially. Or they may subconsciously view achievement as something outside their control – attributing their previous success to luck or other outside factors, and as a result feeling that effort is pointless.

Some learners may experience 'imposter syndrome' – unable to live up to the mantle of giftedness they feel they must wear, they require constant reassurance about their work in order to prevent them comparing it to an impossible ideal. We need to intervene carefully, praising effort but also clarifying the role that personal responsibility plays in success. Often gifted underachievers benefit from guidance with setting goals. Helping them to see a large task as a series of smaller ones can make a big difference.

Twice-exceptional learners

Twice-exceptional learners are an intriguing cohort. They simultaneously present with a gift and a learning difficulty or condition requiring extra specialist support (for example dyslexia, dyscalculia, dysgraphia, ADHD or autism). Any one of these, or a combination of them, could result in unseen challenges. Insightful parents or teachers should be aware of the possibility that a learner may be masking existing learning difficulties. Provide both challenge and support along with increasingly complex and stimulating materials, presented in a multisensory way, to suit their learning strengths.

Most gifted children are similar in many ways to the average child in the classroom, but twice-exceptional learners cause no end of confusion.

Regrettably, teachers may tend to focus more on their difficulties rather than their gifts. It is wise to explore how their gifts could be an avenue to addressing their learning challenges. It also improves a learner's attitude no end when you approach their difficulties via their strengths.

Curriculum provision and teacher practice

Providing an appropriate curriculum for the gifted learner is a major challenge. All the evidence points to the need for something more than mainstream classroom provision. This is not to suggest that this isn't needed – it is, for its normality, the breadth of curriculum delivery, pupil mixing and social learning opportunities – but in addition to that, there need to be enrichment opportunities and social networks for gifted learners to meet, mix and work together. Essentially, a unique type of special education provision is needed for gifted learners, just as for students with learning difficulties, and this should be mandated and resourced centrally.

A responsive and differentiated curriculum for gifted learners needs to be a multi-level, multi-dimensional curriculum that is flexibly accelerated as needs be and allows gifted children to assume ownership of their own learning. And fundamentally, nothing matters more than the quality of the teacher – their open-mindedness towards, awareness of and confidence in the gifted learner. That said, reflecting on the myriad needs and pressures of the mainstream classroom, regardless of how skilled an individual practitioner is, teachers need additional support.

It is time for a more holistic and dedicated response for our gifted learners.

Chapter 26: A last word to parents and carers

No one parenting style is ideal for every gifted learner. Not to dishearten you, but what works well when your gifted child is young is unlikely to work when they are a teen or young adult! As parents we are constantly evolving in tandem with our children, and this is especially necessary as a parent of a gifted learner. Yet if there was one key thing I walked away with from my interviews for this book, it was that many parents of gifted learners are their sons' and daughters' saviours. I saw their enormous struggle to understand their child, to respond to their needs and to advocate for them. The match between parent and child and their mission to support them was often so strong that I felt that no other parent could have parented that specific gifted child. Still, this is not to suggest for a minute that it is easy.

Expert View

"There are only two lasting bequests we can hope to give our children. One of these is roots; the other, wings."

Johann Wolfgang von Goethe

When parenting a gifted learner, raise the young person and not just the gift. Co-journey with your gifted learner as far as you can – and as you are allowed to! Nothing is more important than your relationship – it is first and foremost. Guard it well, and let them know you are there for them and doing your best to understand and facilitate them. Although gifted, they need love, friendship and boundaries. Don't be afraid to put your hands up too and let them know that you may need more from them to better understand them. Discuss their hopes, dreams and goals, and help them to identify a way forward when the breadth of their gifts makes choosing difficult.

Connect with other families with gifted learners. Gifted children need friends with the same interests, and intellectual peers who understand their ideas and get their jokes. Normalise this, where feasible, by socialising with families of other gifted learners. It makes life a bit easier and more normal for parents too. Connect with wider family where possible. It reinforces the child's sense of identity and gives them an extra layer of protection to manage their world. Grandparents are important in the life of the gifted child; they can be more philosophical which can suit their way of thinking.

Give your gifted learner time and be an active listener. Some gifted learners can be quite argumentative, so this may be easier said than done! Communicate that you respect them and are genuinely interested in their thoughts and feelings, but don't lose yourself in the process. Gifted learners need to question critically, so allow time for their questions and where they might lead. Engage positively as your gifted child shares schoolwork with you, using the opportunity to focus on learning rather than grades. They will be noting the messages in what you say.

Because of their uneven development, it is little wonder that gifted learners get confused and feel isolated at times. Acknowledge that this is okay – that this is 'their normal' – and help them to appreciate differences in themselves and others. Model good habits, spend time together, share experiences, and expose them to outdoor and cultural experiences. Notice what they love, follow their interests and let them take the lead. When we match their interests and their passions with learning in and out of school, we're onto a winner. We are handing over the learning to them too.

Never be afraid to advocate for your child's rights. Enlist the support of other parents of gifted learners – nothing changes until it's lobbied for! You will be their life advocate until they become independent and can stand on their own two feet. Liaise with your child's teachers, and offer feedback on home perspectives, your child's interests and wellbeing. Communicate factually and sensitively so it's not taken as a criticism of teacher efforts. Support the school's work to differentiate and provide for extra services where possible.

Finally, mind yourself. You have needs and goals, too. As much as you love your child, don't be a fall guy either! Support yourself by joining a group for parents of gifted learners, online if not locally, and attend any suitable programmes you can link into. As parents it's important that we keep a sense of perspective and realise that there are others in the family too. This was a key message from the interviews.

Above all, give yourself credit for doing your best, and maintain a sense of humour where possible!

Chapter 27: A last word to teachers and schools

It has been a privilege for me to come to know, work with and learn from gifted learners. They are a truly fascinating group in all their genius and vulnerability. Let us not forget that these learners possess a cognitive complexity and depth of thinking that cannot be taught, but like a delicate flower needs to be nurtured, developed and challenged daily. No amount of instruction or practice can instil the cognitive complexity and depth of thinking that our gifted children naturally possess.

> **Key Point**
>
> *No amount of instruction or practice can instil the cognitive complexity and depth of thinking that our gifted children naturally possess.*

Gifted learners are a widely diverse group, in terms of intellectual range, socio-economic backgrounds and social and emotional needs. They deserve a school environment that dispels misconceptions and prejudice and grants them an opportunity for engaged learning and a curriculum that allows them to work with rigour and depth. In Ireland we already know that our top ten percent of students are underperforming; we cannot just presume that they will get by. Left unchallenged they may never realise their potential, and when this happens everyone loses – the learner, their family and society.

Gifted children can be gifted in one area only or across several domains. Teachers need to know that giftedness can manifest unevenly across a pupil's profile, particularly in cases where students might also have undiagnosed learning difficulties (the twice-exceptional learner). Students may feel that their genuine difficulties are being perceived as laziness by teachers or peers who do not understand their uneven presentation of giftedness. Good awareness on the part of teachers protects students from unrealistic expectations, which might compound existing concerns.

Because a gifted learner's brain processes information rapidly, and often thinks in more sophisticated, abstract ways, students need to be challenged at their level to feel valued.[148] Teachers and schools need to be conscious of this when designing instruction. Assess often to find the right entry point. Some suggest that teachers should present the most

---

[148] Venosdale, K. (2011) *Google Plus: What does it mean for education?* Missouri State Teachers Association.

difficult concept first in order to allow advanced learners the opportunity to move onto deeper content, while their peers learn the simpler concepts that lead up to it. The trick is to have other tasks ready that present them with a real challenge. Before differentiating, ensure that you build a class community that celebrates the diversity in the room and facilitates conversations about difference. Avoid labels, use flexible groupings and see what works best.

Give gifted students ownership of their learning. Once a class theme has been introduced (for example sustainability) take suggestions from the gifted students on how it could be developed. Give them responsibility for handling the topic independently and agree a deadline for submission. Let them present their learning to the class for their feedback and analysis. This way everyone is included. This also builds on the principle that gifted students thrive on assignments that let them explore topics of interest in new ways. Authentic, real-life projects are a real draw.

Involve parents in their gifted learner's education. Teachers can sometimes be nervous when communicating with parents. The attitude "we're in this together for your child's benefit" is best. Parents have insights that can help teachers. Gifted children may hold it together and seem focused in class, but can come home very upset or tell parents they are bored. Meanwhile, the teacher's work to accommodate the learner may be unknown to the parent. Sharing lesson intentions and assignments can help to keep everyone in the loop and improve mutual understanding and communication.

Gifted learners deserve fair play in the education system and in law. Recognising giftedness as a unique educational need is essential. It needs to be planned for with adequate resourcing involving dedicated teachers, a reduction in class sizes to allow for more individualised instruction, and differentiation and acceleration supports for gifted and twice-exceptional students. For this to happen, schools, parents, teachers and unions need to work together to move policymakers and legislators. Early intervention is important – young gifted children, sometimes referred to as the 'forgotten children' also need appropriately challenging learning experiences.

Gifted learners should no longer be the poor relation in the education system. When we provide for our gifted learners, we lift all boats. Everyone wins!

Index of *How to Help* advice

Curiosity	35
Problem-solving	43
Avid reading	51
Quick learning	58
Cognitive flexibility	65
Language usage	71
Nurturing creativity	77
Sense of humour	82
Using the TARGET model to engage learners	87
Motivation	89
Managing boredom	93
Embracing boredom	95
Choosing games	100
Dealing with cooperation and conflict	102
Developing leadership abilities	110
Self-esteem	119
Perfectionism	124
Over-excitability and intensity	129
Countdown to exams	134
Stress and anxiety	136
Underachievement	145
The twice-exceptional learner	152
Curriculum modification	155
A differentiated curriculum	158
Best practices for supporting gifted learning	165

Appendices

Appendix 1: Overview of gifted learners interviewed, via Zoom, including parents and teachers

Gifted learner's first name and age	Description	Learner interviewed	Parent interviewed (mother/father)	Teacher interviewed (Female = f; Male = m)	Teaching level of teacher nominated by learner
Primary School/ Elementary School age gifted learners					
Nina (10)	Girl, 4th grade	Yes	Yes (m)	Yes (f)	Primary
Lucy (11)	Girl, 5th grade	Yes	Yes (m)	Yes (f)	Primary
Dylan (12)	Boy, 6th grade	Yes	Yes (m)	Yes (f)	Primary
Jude (12)	Boy, 6th grade	Yes	Yes (f)	Yes (m)	Primary
Secondary level/ High School age gifted learners					
Sasha (17)	Girl, final year	Yes	Yes (f)	Yes (f)	Secondary
Rhys (16)	Boy, 5th year	Yes	Yes (m)	Yes (f)	Primary
Ava (15)	Girl, 3rd year	Yes	Yes (m)	Yes (f)	Primary
Sabrina (15)	Girl, 3rd year	Yes	Yes (m)	Yes (f)	Secondary
Amy (15)	Girl, 3rd year	Yes	Yes (m)	No response	n/a
College/ University level gifted learners					
Luka (24)	Arts Student (Music & French)	Yes	Yes (m)	Yes (f)	Secondary
Ethan (23)	Medicine Student	Yes	Yes (m)	Yes (f)	Primary
Olga (20)	Global Business Student	Yes	Yes (m)	Yes (f)	Primary
Emma (19)	Law & Criminology Student	Yes	Yes (m)	Yes (f)	Secondary
Ruby (24)	Psychology Student	Yes	Yes (m)	Yes (f)	Primary
Adult gifted learners					
Jess (29)	Full-time Mother; Public Health Outreach worker	Yes	Yes (m)	Yes (f)	Primary
Miguel (40)	Paediatrician	Yes	Yes (m)	Yes (f)	Primary
Maria (41)	Engineer	Yes	Yes (m)	No teacher nominated	n/a
Greg (42)	Psychologist and speaker	Yes	Yes (m)	Yes (f)	Secondary
Melissa (58)	Accountant	Yes	No, mother unavailable	Yes (f)	Secondary

Appendix 2: The Gifted Learner Framework (GLF)

The characteristics listed below outline a range of behaviours identified in the gifted literature that are indicative of giftedness.

Important: It is not expected that a learner would demonstrate all of these characteristics.

Learning characteristics	Creativity	Maths and science
The learner shows: ■ Superior reasoning powers ■ Outstanding problem-solving ability ■ Ability to see subtle relationships ■ Persistent intellectual curiosity; questioning ■ Grasp of underlying principles; ability to make generalisations ■ Avid reading, absorbing books well beyond years ■ Ready understanding, quick learning and knowledge retention ■ Flexibility in thinking; considers problems from multiple angles	*The learner shows:* ■ Superior quality and quantity of written and/or spoken vocabulary and usage ■ Creative ability and expression in areas such as music, art, dance, drama, sport ■ Sensitivity and finesse in rhythm, movement, and body control ■ Originality in creative/intellectual work ■ Keen observation and responsiveness to new ideas ■ Alertness, with subtle sense of humour ■ Evidence of divergent thinking	*The learner shows:* ■ Insight into mathematical problems that require careful reasoning ■ Ability to grasp mathematical concepts readily ■ Curiosity about how things work, asks searching questions ■ Ability to grasp scientific concepts readily ■ Enjoyment when working with mathematical and/or scientific concepts
Motivation	**Self-esteem (social and emotional development)**	**Leadership**
The learner shows: ■ Awareness that school is linked to life purpose ■ Outstanding responsibility and independence in classroom work	*The learner shows:* ■ Perfectionism ■ Intensity ■ Over-excitability ■ Self-acceptance, ease and social poise	*The learner shows:* ■ Ability to carry responsibility well ■ Sociability and an outgoing attitude ■ Self-confidence with peers and adults

■ Ability to sustain concentration for long periods of time ■ Initiative in intellectual work ■ Boredom with schoolwork ■ Competitiveness	■ Tendency to be overly self-critical in evaluating/correcting own efforts ■ Ability to set realistically high standards for self ■ Proneness to worry and anxiety ■ Social isolation/loneliness ■ Difficulty 'fitting in' ■ Tendency to be teased and/or bullied	■ Ability to communicate with adults in a mature way ■ Interest in world problems and in solving them ■ Honesty and transparency

© Fidelma Healy Eames, 2020

Appendix 3: Key milestones in gifted education

Adapted from the National Association for Gifted Children (NAGC), the following table shows key dates and milestones in the development of gifted and talented education in the USA and other countries.[1]

Key dates in gifted and talented education in the USA and other countries	
1901	Worcester, Massachusetts, opened the first special school for gifted children.
1916	Lewis Terman, the 'father' of the gifted education movement, publishes the Stanford-Binet, forever changing intelligence testing and the face of American education.
1918	Lulu Stedman establishes an "opportunity room" for gifted students within the University Training School at the Southern Branch of the University of California.
1921	Lewis Terman begins what has remained the longest running longitudinal study of gifted children with an original sample of 1,500 gifted children.
1925	Lewis Terman publishes *Genetic Studies of Genius*, concluding that gifted students are: a. qualitatively different in school b. slightly better physically and emotionally in comparison to normal students c. superior in academic subjects in comparison to the average students d. emotionally stable e. most successful when education and family values were held in high regard by the family f. infinitely variable in combination with the number of traits exhibited by those in the study. This is the first volume in a five-volume study spanning nearly 40 years.
1926	Leta Hollingworth publishes *Gifted Children: Their Nature and Nurture*, considered to be the first textbook on gifted education.
1936	Hollingworth establishes P. S. 500, the Speyer School, for gifted children ages 7-9.

---

[1] NAGC (2005) *The History of Gifted and Talented Education*. National Association for Gifted Children [online].

Key dates in gifted and talented education in the USA and other countries

1954 — The National Association of Gifted Children is founded under the leadership of Ann Isaacs.

1957 — **Russia:** The Soviet Union launches Sputnik, sparking the United States to re-examine its human capital and the quality of American schooling, particularly in mathematics and science.
As a result, substantial amounts of money pour into identifying the brightest and most talented students who would best profit from advanced math, science and technology programming.

1958 — The National Defence Education Act passes. This is the first large-scale effort in gifted education by the federal government.

1972 — The Marland Report – The first formal definition is issued encouraging schools to define giftedness broadly. Along with academic and intellectual talent, the definition includes leadership ability, visual and performing arts, creative or productive thinking, and psychomotor ability.
[*Note: psychomotor ability was excluded from subsequent revisions of the federal definition.*]

1974 — The Office of the Gifted and Talented housed within the U.S. Office of Education is given official status.

1975 — Public Law 94-142 The Education for all Handicapped Children Act establishes a federal mandate to serve children with special education needs but does not include children with gifts and talents.

1978 — **Australia:** Activity on behalf of gifted learners rose dramatically in several Australian states since 1978. However, the most exciting, challenging and worthwhile innovations have occurred in Western Australia where recognition has been given to special programmes.

1983 — *A Nation at Risk* reports scores of America's brightest students and their failure to compete with international counterparts. The report includes policies and practices in gifted education, raising academic standards and promoting appropriate curriculum for gifted learners.

1988 — Congress passes the Jacob Javits Gifted and Talented Students Education Act as part of the Reauthorization of the Elementary and Secondary Education Act.

1988 — The European Council of High Ability (ECHA) established as a European NGO. Its major aim is to promote the exchange of information between people interested in high ability – teachers, researchers, psychologists, parents, politicians and the highly able themselves.

Key dates in gifted and talented education in the USA and other countries

1990	The National Research Center on the Gifted and Talented was established at the University of Connecticut and included researchers at the University of Virginia, Yale University, and the University of Georgia. [*Note: funding for the NRC ended in 2012*]
1993	*National Excellence: The Case for Developing America's Talent*, issued by the US Department of Education, outlines how America neglects its most talented youth. The report also makes a number of recommendations influencing the last decade of research in the field of gifted education.
1993	**Ireland:** In 1993 the Centre for Talented Youth in Ireland (CTYI) ran its first summer programme for gifted children in secondary school using students identified from a Talent Search. In the first year of the programme, 133 Irish students attended.
1997	**UK:** In 1997 the UK Government launched the Gifted & Talented strategy.
1999	**UK:** In 1999 policy development efforts in UK education required that teachers select gifted and talented pupils and, by making appropriate educational provision, steer them along the gifted education highway.[2]
1998	NAGC publishes Pre-K-Grade 12 Gifted Program Standards to provide guidance in seven key areas for programs serving gifted and talented students. The standards were revised in 2010 as Pre-K-Grade 12 Gifted Programming Standards.
2000	**Scotland:** Standards in Scotland's Schools (2000) Act supports an egalitarian ethos that permeates Scottish education. The belief that education is a right for all foreshadows Scotland's approach to "gifted education". The legislative shift within Scotland from a "needs-based" model to a "rights-based" model, coupled with an inclusive approach to education for all, provides potential opportunities for gifted young people.[3]
2002	The *No Child Left Behind Act* (NCLB) (2001) is passed as the reauthorisation of the Elementary and Secondary Education Act. The Javits program is included in NCLB, and expanded to offer competitive state-wide grants. The definition of gifted and talented students is modified again: *Students, children, or youth who give evidence of high achievement capability in areas such as intellectual, creative, artistic, or leadership capacity, or in specific academic fields, and who need services and activities not ordinarily provided by the school in order to fully develop those capabilities.*

2 Casey, R. & Koshy, V. (2013) Gifted and Talented Education: The English Policy Highway at a Crossroads? *Journal for the Education of the Gifted*. 36, 44-65.
3 Sutherland, M., and Stack, N. (2014) Ability as an additional support need: Scotland's inclusive approach to gifted education. *Centre for Educational Policy Studies Journal*, 4(3). 73-87.

2004	*A Nation Deceived: How Schools Hold Back America's Brightest Students*[4], a national research-based report on acceleration strategies for advanced learners is published by the Belin-Blank Centre at the University of Iowa.
2006	NAGC publishes national gifted education standards for teacher preparation programs and knowledge and skill standards in gifted education for all teachers. The standards were revised in 2013.
2007	**Ireland:** National draft guidelines are produced for teachers of exceptionally able pupils.
2013	**Finland:** In Finland's education system there are no laws that grant special education for gifted students. However, due to the value Finland places on education, individualism and freedom of choice, students are educated according to their talents, an approach that is the main goal of gifted education. Some schools accept small numbers of students, for example International Baccalaureate programmes and some schools are also based more on science and mathematics learning.[5]

---

4   Colangelo, N., Assouline, S.G. & Gross, M.U.M. (2004) *A Nation Deceived: How Schools Hold Back America's Brightest Students. The Templeton National Report on Acceleration. Volume 2.* Connie Belin & Jacqueline N. Blank International Center for Gifted Education and Talent Development.

5   Tirri, K. & Kuusisto, E. (2013) How Finland Serves Gifted and Talented Pupils. *Journal for the Education of the Gifted*, 36(1), 84-96.

Appendix 4: High Achiever, Gifted Learner, Creative Thinker Comparator[30]

A High Achiever...	A Gifted Learner...	A Creative Thinker...
Remembers the answers.	Poses unforeseen questions.	Sees exceptions.
Is interested.	Is curious.	Wonders.
Is attentive.	Is selectively mentally engaged.	Daydreams; may seem off task.
Generates advanced ideas.	Generates complex, abstract ideas.	Overflows with ideas, many of which will never be developed.
Works hard to achieve.	Knows without working hard.	Plays with ideas and concepts.
Answer the questions in detail.	Ponders with depth and multiple perspectives.	Injects new possibilities.
Performs at the top of the group.	Is beyond the group.	Is in own group.
Responds with interest and opinions.	Exhibits feelings and opinions from multiple perspectives.	Shares bizarre, sometimes conflicting opinions.
Learns with ease.	Already knows.	Questions: What if...?
Needs 6 to 8 repetitions to master.	Needs 1 to 3 repetitions to master.	Questions the need for mastery.
Comprehends at a high level.	Comprehends in-depth, complex ideas.	Overflows with ideas, many of which will never be developed.
Enjoys the company of age peers.	Prefers the company of intellectual peers.	Prefers the company of creative peers but often works alone.

A High Achiever...	A Gifted Learner...	A Creative Thinker...
Understands complex, abstract humour.	Creates complex, abstract humour.	Relishes wild, off-the-wall humour.
Grasps meaning.	Infers and connects concepts.	Makes mental leaps: Aha!
Completes assignments on time.	Initiates projects and extensions of assignments.	Initiates more projects than will ever be completed.
Is receptive.	Is intense.	Is independent and unconventional.
Is accurate and complete.	Is original and continually developing.	Is original and continually developing.
Enjoys school often.	Enjoys self-directed learning.	Enjoys creating.
Absorbs information.	Manipulates information.	Improvises.
Is a technician with expertise in a field.	Is an expert who abstracts beyond the field.	Is an inventor and idea generator.
Memorises well.	Guesses and infers well.	Creates and brainstorms well.
Is highly alert and observant.	Anticipates and relates observations.	Is intuitive.
Is pleased with own learning.	Is self-critical.	Is never finished with possibilities.
Gets A's.	May not be motivated by grades.	May not be motivated by grades.
Is able.	Is intellectual.	Is idiosyncratic.

Appendix 5: Giftedness/Autism Spectrum Disorder Level 1 Checklist[1]

Gifted	Autism Spectrum Disorder Level 1
Memory and Attention	
■ Excellent memory for facts and information about a variety of topics ■ Typically accurate recall for names and faces ■ Dislikes rote memorization tasks although he/she may do it well ■ Intense focus on topics of interest ■ If distracted, is likely to return to a task quickly with or without redirection	■ Superb memory for facts and detailed information related to selected topics of special interest ■ Poor recall for names and faces ■ Enjoys thinking about and remembering details, facts, and figures ■ Intense focus on primary topic of interest ■ If distracted by internal thoughts, redirecting to task at hand may be difficult
Speech and Language	
■ Extensive, advanced vocabulary ■ Communicates understandings of abstract ideas ■ Rich and interesting verbal style ■ Engages others in interests ■ Asks challenging questions ■ Expressive language/speech pattern of an older child ■ Elaborates with or without prompts ■ Understands and engages in sophisticated and/or socially reciprocal humor, irony, and sarcasm ■ Understands cause/effect or give and take of conversation ■ Able to communicate distress verbally	■ Advanced use of words with lack of comprehension for all language used ■ Thinks and communicates in concrete and literal terms with less abstraction ■ Uninviting verbal style ■ Style or content lacks reciprocity and engagement of others in their personal interests ■ Repeats questions and information ■ Pedantic and seamless speech ■ Little or no elaboration with run-on speech ■ Misunderstands jokes involving social reciprocity ■ Has difficulty understanding give and take of conversation ■ Communicates distress with actions rather than words
Social and Emotional	
■ Able to identify and name friends; enjoys high social status in some circles ■ Aware of social norms ■ Keenly aware that he/she is different from peers	■ Demonstrates significant difficulty and lacks understanding of how to establish and keep friends ■ Indifferent to social norms of dress and behavior ■ Limited recognition of differences with peers

---

1   Amend, E.R., Beaver-Gavin, K., Schuler, P. & Beights, R. (2008) *Giftedness/Asperger's Disorder Checklist (GADC) Pre-Referral Checklist*. Amend Psychological Services [online].

■ Spontaneous sharing of enjoyment, activities, interests, or accomplishments ■ Engages others in conversation ■ Aware of another's perspective and able to take and understand others' viewpoint ■ Follows unwritten rules of social interactions ■ Shows keen social insight and an intuitive nature ■ Usually demonstrates appropriate emotions ■ Aware of others' emotions and recognizes others' feelings easily ■ Able to read social situations and respond to social cues ■ Shows empathy for others and able to comfort a friend in need	■ Little or no interest in spontaneous sharing of enjoyment, activities, interests, or accomplishments ■ Shows significant difficulty initiating or engaging others in conversation ■ Assume others share his/her personal views ■ Unaware of social conventions or the reasons behind them ■ Lacks social insight ■ Demonstrates inappropriate or immature emotions and flat or restricted affect ■ Limited recognition of others' emotions ■ Misreads social situations and may not respond (or even know how to respond) to social cues ■ Does not typically show empathy or concern for someone in need
Behavioral	
■ May passively resist but will often go along with change ■ Questions rules and structure ■ Stereotypical behaviors (e.g., hand or finger flapping, twisting, or complex body movements) not present ■ When problems arise, he/she is typically distressed by them	■ Actively or aggressively resists change; rigid ■ Adheres strictly to rules and needs structure ■ Stereotypical behaviors (e.g., hand or finger flapping, twisting, or complex body movements) are present ■ When problems arise, parents or teachers are distressed by them while student may be unaware of distressing situation unless personally affected
Motor Skills	
■ Well-coordinated ■ Interested in team sports ■ Demonstrates appropriate development of self-help skills	■ Lacks age-appropriate coordination ■ Avoids team sports ■ Delayed acquisition of self-help skills

From Amend, Beaver-Gavin, Schuler, and Beights (2008).

Appendix 6: Schedule of questions used to interview the gifted learner

Gifted learner interview questions

Learner's name: _____ Date of birth: _____

Parent's name _____ Heritage: _____

Parents' occupations: _____

Stage you're at: _____

> 1. Use the Gifted Learner Framework as a reference to think about yourself, to identify some stand-out features about yourself, to help the author establish a picture of you as a learner.

> 2. Reflect on what helped you and fulfilled you as a learner – the activities, the challenges, the events, the people (e.g. parents, teachers, others) and why.

> 3. Reflect on what didn't help you as a learner and why.

4. Do you think that your 'giftedness' has changed over time and, if so, how?

5. What advice would you give to parents and educators of gifted children/students?

6. Any other comments you would like to add?

Thank you for your contribution to this Gifted Learner study.

Appendix 7: Schedule of questions used to interview parents of gifted learners

Parent Interview Questions

Child's name: _____ Date of birth: _____

Parent's name _____ Heritage: _____

Parents' occupations: _____

1. Use the Gifted Learner Framework as a reference to reflect on, and identify some stand-out features about your child – their strengths and challenges.

2. Reflect, in particular, on what helped to fulfil him/her as a learner, in your view – the activities, the challenges, the events, the people (e.g. teachers, others) and why.

3. Reflect on ways, unique to their needs, that you helped him/her as a parent – Did your notice, for example, that your child's 'giftedness' changed over time?

4. Consider when s/he experienced particular challenges and how you addressed them – for example, were there times you could have used help in your child's life?

5. What advice would you give to other parents of gifted learners?

6. Any other comments you would like to add?

Thank you for your contribution to this Gifted Learner study.

Appendix 8: Schedule of questions used to interview teachers of gifted learners

Teacher Interview Questions

Student name: _____ Date of birth: _____

Teacher's name _____

1. Use the Gifted Learner Framework as a reference to reflect on, and identify some stand-out features about your gifted learner – their strengths and challenges. Circle the characteristics on the framework that apply to your gifted learner.

2. Reflect, in particular, on what helped to fulfil him/her as a learner, in your view – the activities, the challenges, the events, the people that you know of and why.

3. Reflect on ways, unique to their needs, that you helped him/her as a teacher. Did you notice, for example, that his/her 'giftedness' changed over time?

4. Consider when s/he experienced particular challenges and how you addressed them – for example, were there times you could have used more help/ guidance?

5. What advice would you give to parents of gifted learners?

6. Does the state government (e.g. Dept. of Education/ Health) adequately address the needs of gifted learners? What would you recommend to help teachers with gifted learners?

Thank you for your contribution to this Gifted Learner study.

Appendix 9: Resources

This is a guide to resources referred to within this book that you may find helpful for gifted learners.

Assessment and Tests

- Ahmann, J. S. (1985). Otis-Lennon School Ability Test. Measurement and Evaluation in Counseling and Development, 17(4), 226–229. https://doi.org/10.1080/07481756.1985.12022780
- Assessment (NCCA), N. C. for C. and. (2007). NCCA [System.String[]]. NCCA; National Council for Curriculum and Assessment (NCCA). https://ncca.ie/en/primary/assessment/
- Atwell, N., Boman, M., Borland, P., Duarte, M., Fishback, L., Miller, C., & Romero, E. (2008). Read & Write Gold: Technology Increasing Student Achievement.
- Faupel, A. (2003). Emotional literacy: Assessment and intervention: ages 11 to 16. User's guide. GL Assessment.
- Gifted Assessments | Online Gifted Screening Test. (n.d.). Advanced Psychology. Retrieved October 21, 2021, from https://www.psy-ed.com/wpblog/gifted-assessments/index.php
- Hamhuis, E., Glas, C., & Meelissen, M. (2020). Tablet assessment in primary education: Are there performance differences between TIMSS' paper-and-pencil test and tablet test among Dutch grade-four students? British Journal of Educational Technology, 51(6), 2340–2358. https://doi.org/10.1111/bjet.12914
- Iowa Test | Assessments and ITBS Test (2021 Update)—TestingMom.com. (n.d.). Testing Mom. Retrieved December 20, 2021, from https://www.testingmom.com/tests/itbs-test/
- Maths Admissions Test | Mathematical Institute. (n.d.). Retrieved December 20, 2021, from https://www.maths.ox.ac.uk/study-here/undergraduate-study/maths-admissions-test
- NAGC. (n.d.). Tests & Assessments | National Association for Gifted Children. Retrieved October 1, 2021, from https://www.nagc.org/resources-publications/gifted-education-practices/identification/tests-assessments
- Naglieri Nonverbal Ability Test | Third Edition. (n.d.). Retrieved December 20, 2021, from https://www.pearsonassessments.com/store/usassessments/en/Store/Professional-Assessments/Cognition-%26-

- Neuro/Non-Verbal-Ability/Naglieri-Nonverbal-Ability-Test-%7C-Third-Edition/p/100001822.html
- O'Mahoney, A., & Ryan, R. M. C. (2018). SALF: Self Assessment and Learning Folders. Outside the Box Learning Resources. https://www.otb.ie/shop/salf-resources/
- Reynolds, M. R., & Niileksela, C. R. (2015). Test Review: Schrank, F. A., McGrew, K. S., & Mather, N. (2014). Woodcock-Johnson IV Tests of Cognitive Abilities. Journal of Psychoeducational Assessment, 33(4), 381–390. https://doi.org/10.1177/0734282915571408
- SAGES-2 Test Overview—TestingMom.com. (n.d.). TestingMom. Retrieved December 20, 2021, from https://www.testingmom.com/tests/sages-2-test/
- SAT. (2016, November 28). SAT Suite of Assessments. https://collegereadiness.collegeboard.org/sat
- Standardized Test, SRA Reading and Arithmetic Indices | National Museum of American History. (n.d.). Retrieved December 20, 2021, from https://americanhistory.si.edu/collections/search/object/nmah_1213730
- Test of Nonverbal Intelligence | Fourth Edition. (n.d.). Retrieved December 20, 2021, from https://www.pearsonassessments.com/store/usassessments/en/Store/Professional-Assessments/Cognition-%26-Neuro/Non-Verbal-Ability/Test-of-Nonverbal-Intelligence-%7C-Fourth-Edition/p/100000612.html
- WikiJob Team. (2021, September). The CAT4 Cognitive Abilities Test: Guide & Practice Questions. https://www.wikijob.co.uk/content/aptitude-tests/school-assessment-tests/the-cat4-cognitive-abilities-test

Curriculum-related resources – teachers and parents

- Bate, J., & Clark, D. (2012). Gifted Kids Curriculum: What do the Students Say? 13(2), 6.
- Bate, J., Clark, D., & Riley, T. (2012). Gifted Kids Curriculum: What Do the Students Say? Kairaranga, 13(2), 23–28.
- Katz, J. (2013). UDL & Gifted Education. Jennifer Katz, PhD. https://www.ThreeBlockModel.com/udl--gifted-education.html
- Kingore, B. (2004). High achiever, gifted learner, creative learner. Understanding Our Gifted, 16(3), 21.
- Maker, C. J., & Nielson, A. B. (1996). Curriculum Development and Teaching Strategies for Gifted Learners. Second Edition. PRO-ED, 8700 Shoal Creek Blvd.

- Porter, L. (2020). Gifted Young Children: A guide for teachers and parents. https://doi.org/10.4324/9781003115816
- Tips for Teaching Gifted Students | Scholastic. (n.d.). Retrieved December 15, 2021, from http://www.scholastic.com/teachers/articles/teaching-content/tips-teaching-gifted-students/
- Universal design for learning. (n.d.). Universal Design for Learning. Retrieved September 22, 2021, from http://easternshoreudl.weebly.com/brain-networks.html
- Webb, J. T., Gore, J. L., & Amend, E. R. (2007). A Parent's Guide to Gifted Children. Great Potential Press, Inc.
- Winebrenner, S., & Espeland, P. (1992). Teaching Gifted Kids in the Regular Classroom: Strategies and Techniques Every Teacher Can Use To Meet the Academic Needs of the Gifted and Talented. Free Spirit Publishing, Inc.
- Weisbord, M., & Janoff, S. (2010). Future Search: Getting the Whole System in the Room for Vision, Commitment, and Action. Berrett-Koehler Publishers.

Play

- How to Engage in Play With Your Children – and Enjoy It. (2016, January 10). Child Psychology Resources by Dr. Tali Shenfield. https://www.psy-ed.com/wpblog/play-with-your-children/

Cooperative Games

- Family Pastimes Cooperative Games—Fun Boardgames for Everyone. (n.d.). Family Pastimes Cooperative Games. Retrieved November 13, 2021, from https://familypastimes.com/

Reading-related resources

- Accelerated Reader Bookfinder US. (n.d.). Retrieved December 15, 2021, from https://www.arbookfind.com/UserType.aspx?RedirectURL=%2fdefault.aspx
- Brown, K., & Brown, J. "Rachel." (2019). I Am Perfectly Designed. Henry Holt and Company (BYR).
- Burningham, J. (2002). Granpa. Red Fox.
- O'Neal, E. (2017, September 19). Got a gifted reader? Here are an educator's top tips for story time. Pick Any Two. https://pickanytwo.net/engaging-gifted-readers/

Vocabulary

- Jen. (n.d.). Teaching Vocabulary to Gifted and Advanced Learners—Instructional Strategies that Work—Soaring with Snyder. Soaring with Snyder. Retrieved October 21, 2021, from https://www.soaringwithsnyder.com/2018/02/teaching-vocabulary-to-gifted-and.html
- Rasinski et. al (2020). Building Vocabulary with Greek and Latin Roots. Shell Education.
- Rasinski (2005) Daily Word Ladders: 100 Reproducible Word Study Lessons That Help Kids Boost Reading, Vocabulary, Spelling and Phonics – Independently! Scholastic US.
- Giddens (2005). Word Puzzles for Really Busy Teachers. www.otb.ie.

Self-Esteem

- Big Life Journal: Growth Mindset for Kids & Teens. (n.d.). Retrieved November 21, 2021, from https://biglifejournal.com/
- Boorman, H., & Kottmeyer, C. (2018). The Gifted Kids Workbook: Mindfulness Skills to Help Children Reduce Stress, Balance Emotions, and Build Confidence (Workbook edition). Instant Help.
- Borba, M. (1994). The Building Blocks of Self-esteem. Jalmar Press.
- Brennan, F. (2021). The Self-Love Habit: Transform fear and self-doubt into serenity, peace and power. Gill & Macmillan Ltd.
- Burton, N. (2014, July 30). The Surprising Benefits of Boredom | Psychology Today. https://www.psychologytoday.com/us/blog/hide-and-seek/201407/the-surprising-benefits-boredom
- Byers, G. (2018). I Am Enough. HarperCollins.
- Gelb, M. J. (2013). Body Learning: An Introduction to the Alexander Technique. Aurum.
- Open Heart Meditation. (n.d.). Open Heart Meditation TM. Retrieved November 23, 2021, from https://www.openheartmeditation.com/
- Rigsbee, C. (2018, September 4). Strategies for Helping Stressed-Out Gifted Learners. https://blogs.tip.duke.edu/teachersworkshop/strategies-for-helping-stressed-out-gifted-learners/
- Schultz, J. (n.d.). Social Anxiety in Kids: What You Need to Know. Retrieved November 23, 2021, from https://www.understood.org/articles/en/social-anxiety-and-learning-and-thinking-differences-what-you-need-to-know
- Wilson, H. E., & Adelson, J. L. (2018). Perfectionism: Helping Gifted Children Learn Healthy Strategies and Create Realistic Expectations. Parenting for High Potential, 7(3), 8.

Career Guidance

- Career Challenge Cards—Study and Careers Galway. (n.d.). Retrieved October 26, 2021, from https://studyandcareers.ie/product/single-challenge-cards-deck/

Maths

- Khan Academy | Free Online Courses, Lessons & Practice. (n.d.). Retrieved December 15, 2021, from https://www.khanacademy.org/

Study Skills

- Potash, B. (2017, October 18). Sketchnotes in the Classroom: 8 Ideas to Get Started. WeAreTeachers. https://www.weareteachers.com/use-sketchnotes-in-the-classroom/
- Study and Career Guidance Galway. (n.d.). Retrieved November 13, 2021, from https://studyandcareers.ie/
- Switching on for Learning: Becoming an Independent Learner - Online Course - Study and Careers Galway. (n.d.). Retrieved October 21, 2021, from https://studyandcareers.ie/switching-on-for-learning/

Science

- R, K. (2019, February 15). SOF Science Olympiad Syllabus | Download SOF NSO Syllabus 2021. GetMyUni. https://www.getmyuni.com/olympiad/nso-national-science-olympiad-syllabus
- Science Olympiad. (n.d.). Retrieved December 15, 2021, from https://www.soinc.org/

Gifted Centres

- Centre for Talented Youth, Ireland | Dublin City University |. (n.d.). Retrieved November 13, 2021, from https://www.dcu.ie/ctyi

References

Addison, L. (1985). *Leadership Skills Among the Gifted and Talented*, 1985 Digest. ERIC Clearinghouse for Disabilities and Gifted Education [online].

Amabile, T.M. (1983) The social psychology of creativity: A componential conceptualization. *Journal of Personality and Social Psychology* 45(2) 357-376.

Amend, E.R., Beaver-Gavin, K., Schuler, P. & Beights, R. (2008) *Giftedness/Asperger's Disorder Checklist (GADC) Pre-Referral Checklist*. Amend Psychological Services [online].

Amend, E.R., Schuler, P., Beaver-Gavin, K. & Beights, R. (2009) A Unique Challenge: Sorting Out the Differences between Giftedness and Asperger's Disorder. *Gifted Child Today*, 32(4), 57-63.

Bainbridge, C. (2020) *Are Children Gifted If They Learn How to Read Earlier Than Others?* Verywell Family [online].

Bainbridge, C. (2020) *How to Motivate Your Gifted Child*. Verywell Family [online].

Bainbridge, C. (2021) *How Learning to Read Without Instruction Relates to Giftedness*. Verywell Family [online].

Bainbridge, C. (2021) *Underachievement in Gifted Children*. Verywell Family [online].

Banks, F. & Mayes, A.S. (2001) *Early Professional Development for Teachers*. David Fulton.

Bate, J., Clark, D. & Riley, T. (2012) Gifted Kids Curriculum: What Do the Students Say? *Kairaranga*, 13(2) 23-28.

Baum, S.M. (1994). Meeting the Needs of Gifted/Learning Disabled Students: How Far Have We Come? *Journal of Secondary Gifted Education*, 5(3), 6-22.

Baum, S. & Owen, S.V. (1988) High Ability/Learning Disabled Students: How Are They Different? *Gifted Child Quarterly*, 32(3), 321-326.

Bélanger, J. & Gagné, F. (2006). Estimating the Size of the Gifted/Talented Population from Multiple Identification Criteria. *Journal for the Education of the Gifted* 30 (2), 131-163.

Bergen, D. (2009) Gifted children's humor preferences, sense of humor, and Comprehension of riddles. Humor: *International Journal of Humor Research* 22(4) 419-436.

Berger, S.L. (1991) *Differentiating curriculum for gifted students*. Davidson Institute [online].

Berliner, W. (2017) Why there's no such thing as a gifted child. *The Guardian* [online].

Bloom, B.S. (1956) *Taxonomy of educational objectives*. David McKay.

Bond, C.F. & Titus, L.J. (1983) Social facilitation: A meta-analysis of 241 studies. *Psychological Bulletin*, 94(2), 265-292.

Boorman, H. & Kottmeyer, C. (2018) *The Gifted Kids Workbook: Mindfulness Skills to Help Children Reduce Stress, Balance Emotions, and Build Confidence*. New Harbinger.

Borba, M. (1989) Esteem Builders. A K-8 *Self- Esteem Curriculum for Improving Student Achievement, Behavior and School Climate*. Jalmar Press

Borland, J.H. [ed] (2003) *Rethinking Gifted Education*; Teacher's College Press

Bradley, T. (2006) *Chill Out: Helping Gifted Youth Deal with Stress*. TerryBradleyGifted [online].

Brown, E.F. (2015) Serving Gifted Students in General Ed Classrooms. *Edutopia* [online].

Brown, K., Brown, J. & Syed, A. (2020) *I Am Perfectly Designed*. Macmillan.

Brown, T.T. (2012) *Brain Development During the Preschool Years*. SpringerLink [online].

Burningham, J. (2003) *Granpa*. Red Fox

Byers, G. & Bobo, K.A. (2020) *I Am Enough*. BalzerBray.

Caldwell, J. (1998) How to identify and nurture our gifted children'. *Independent*.ie [online].

Casey, R. & Koshy, V. (2013) Gifted and Talented Education: The English Policy Highway at a Crossroads? *Journal for the Education of the Gifted*. 36, 44-65.

CCI (2019) *Perfectionism in Perspective*. Centre for Clinical Interventions [online].

CDC (2022) *What is Cerebral Palsy?* Centers for Disease Control and Prevention.

Cecchini, J., Fernandez-Rio, J., Méndez-Giménez, A., Cecchini, C. & Martins, L. (2014) Epstein's TARGET Framework and Motivational Climate in Sport: Effects of a Field-Based, Long-Term Intervention Program. *International Journal of Sports Science & Coaching* 9(6): 1325-1340.

Clancy, R. (2021) Cill Rialaig Arts Centre

Clinkenbeard, P.R. (2012). Motivation and gifted students: Implications of theory and research. *Psychology in the Schools*, 49(7), 622-630.

Colangelo, N., Assouline, S.G. & Gross, M.U.M. (2004) *A Nation Deceived: How Schools Hold Back America's Brightest Students. The Templeton National Report on Acceleration. Volume 2*. Connie Belin & Jacqueline N. Blank International Center for Gifted Education and Talent Development.

Colangelo, N. & Davis, G.A. (2002) *Handbook on Gifted Education*, 3rd ed. Allyn & Bacon

Cole, P. (2016) 10 Fun Web Apps, Games, for Teaching Critical Thinking Skills. EmergingEdTech [online].

Columbus Group (1991) Unpublished transcript of the meeting of the Columbus Group, cited in Silverman, L.K. (1997). The Construct of Asynchronous Development. *Peabody Journal of Education*, 72(3&4), 36-58.

Cornell, D.G. (1989) Child Adjustment and Parent Use of the Term "Gifted". *Gifted Child Quarterly* 33(2).

Dally, P. & Gomez, J. (1979) Capgras: Case study and reappraisal of psychopathology. *British Journal of Medical Psychology* 52(3) 291-295.

Daniels, S. & Piechowski, M.M. (2009) *Living with Intensity: Understanding the Sensitivity, Excitability, and Emotional Development of Gifted Children, Adolescents and Adults*. Gifted Unlimited.

Das, P. (2019) *Curiosity and passion are the keys to become a scientist… we need to create an environment that nurtures research*. Times of India Blog [online].

David, H. (2011) Teachers' Attitude: Its importance in nurturing and educating gifted children. *Gifted and Talented International*, 26(1-2), 65-80.

David, H. (2019). Learning Disabilities, Attention Deficit (Hyperactivity) Disorder, and Intelligence. *Davidson Institute*, 13.

Davis, G.A. & Rimm, S.B. (1985). *Education of the Gifted and Talented*. 5th ed. Pearson.

Delaune, A. (2016) Emotional, social, and relationship development for gifted and talented children in early childhood education. *He Kupu*, 4.

Dirkes, M.A. (1983) Anxiety in the gifted: Pluses and minuses. *Roeper Review* 6(2) 68-70.

Eide, B.L. & Eide, F.F. (2006) The Mislabeled Child. *The New Atlantis* [online].

Engel, S. (2015) *The Hungry Mind: The Origins of Curiosity in Childhood*. Harvard University Press.

Eren, F., Çete, A.Ö., Avcil, S. & Baykara, B. (2018) Emotional and Behavioral Characteristics of Gifted Children and Their Families. *Archives of Neuropsychiatry* 55(2) 105-112.

Escalante, A. (2018) Boredomtunity: Why Boredom Is the Best Thing for Our Kids. *Psychology Today*. [online].

Eva Machů, E., Kočvarová, I. & Kopřivovác, R. (2016) Tendencies of gifted pupils toward selected aspects of conformist behavior in the context of their relationships with classmates. *Procedia - Social and Behavioral Sciences* 217, 214-221.

Faupel, A. (2003) *Emotional literacy: Assessment and intervention: ages 11 to 16. User's guide*. GL Assessment.

Feldhusen, J. (2001) Through Another's Eyes: The Role of Grandparents in Talent Recognition and Development. *Gifted Child Today* 24(3) 25-65.

Gagne, F. (2000) *A Differentiated Model of Giftedness and Talent*. Year 2000 Update. ERIC [online].

Galbraith, J. & Delisle, J. (2015) *When Gifted Kids Don't Have All the Answers: How to Meet Their Social and Emotional Needs*. Free Spirit Publishing.

Garner, D. (1991) Eating disorders in the gifted adolescent. In Bireley, M. & Genshaft, J. (1991) *Understanding the Gifted Adolescent* pp. 50-64. Teacher's College Press.

Giger, M. (2006) *The Munich Model of Giftedness* [online].

Gindi, S., Kohan-Mass, J. & Pilipel, A. (2019) Gender Differences in Competition Among Gifted Students: The Role of Single-Sex Versus Co-Ed Classrooms. *Roeper Review* 41(3) 199-210.

Gottfried, A.W., Gottfried, A.E., Bathurst, K. & Guerin, D.W. (1994) *Gifted IQ: Early Developmental Aspects – The Fullerton Longitudinal Study*. Springer.

Grier, J.E. (2020) *Effectively Implementing Gifted Education for Overlooked Students in PA: Examination and Recommendations for Modification of PA. Code 22 Ch. 16*. ERIC [online].

Gross, G. (2013) Who Is the Gifted Child? *HuffPost Life* [online].

Heller, K.A., Perleth, C. & Lim, T.K. (2005) The Munich Model of Giftedness Designed to Identify and Promote Gifted Students. *In Conceptions of Giftedness*, 2nd ed (pp. 147-170). Cambridge University Press.

Heshmat, S. (2020) 5 Benefits of Boredom. *Psychology Today* [online].

https://studyandcareers.ie/inspiring-ireland/

ttps://studyandcareers.ie/switching-on-for-learning/

Institute for Educational Advancement (2012). *5 Definitions of Giftedness*. [online]

Johnson, D.W., & Johnson, R.T. (1987). *Learning together and alone: Cooperative, competitive, and individualistic learning*, 2nd ed (pp. xiii, 193). Prentice-Hall.

Joslyn, N. (2022) *Gifted Kids and Competition*. Family Education [online].

Kadioglu, C. & Uzuntiryaki, E. (2008) *Motivational Factors Contributing to Turkish High School Students' Achievement in Gases and Chemical Reactions*. ERIC [online].

Kao, C.-Y. (2011) The dilemma of competition encountered by musically gifted Asian male students: An exploration from the perspective of gifted education. *High Ability Studies* 22(1) 19-42.

Karnes, F.A. & Bean, S.M. (1990) *Developing Leadership in Gifted Youth*. ERIC Clearinghouse for Disabilities and Gifted Education [online].

Kashdan, T. & Silvia, P. (2009) Curiosity and Interest: The Benefits of Thriving on Novelty and Challenge. In *Oxford Handbook of Positive Psychology*, Oxford University Press.

Katz, J. (2013) *UDL & Gifted Education* Threeblockmodel.com [online].

Katz, J. (2013) *UDL & Gifted Education: Who Are Gifted Learners?* [online].

Kaufman, S.B. (2017) *Schools Are Missing What Matters About Learning*. The Atlantic [online].

Kennedy-Moore, E. (2012) *Helping Gifted Children Handle Cooperation and Competition*. Davidson Institute [online].

Khalil, M. & Accariya, Z. (2016) Identifying "Good" Teachers for Gifted Students. *Creative Education*, 7, 407-418.

Kingore, B. (2003) High Achiever, Gifted Learner, Creative Thinker. *Understanding Our Gifted*, 15, 3-5.

Kingore, B. (2004) *High Achiever, Gifted Learner, Creative Learner* [online].

Kingore, B. (2004). High achiever, gifted learner, creative learner. *Understanding Our Gifted*, 16(3), 21.

Kočvarová, I., Machů, E. & Petrujová, J. (2016) Self-assessment of teachers working with gifted pupils in terms of their work experience and education. In: *ICERI2016*: 9th

Kottmeyer, C. (2020). *Never Say Bored!* Hoagies Gifted Education Page [online].

Kuo, C.-C., Maker, J., Su, F.-L. & Hu, C. (2010) Identifying young gifted children and cultivating problem solving abilities and multiple intelligences. *Learning and Individual Differences* 20(4) 365-379.

LaChance, N. (2016). *Social Self-Esteem and Gifted Kids*. Institute for Educational Advancement [online].

Lee, S.-Y. & Olszewski-Kubilius, P. (2016) Leadership Development and Gifted Students. In R. J. R. Levesque (Ed.), *Encyclopedia of Adolescence*. Springer International Publishing.

Li, A.K.F. & Adamson, G. (1992) Gifted Secondary Students' Preferred Learning Style: Cooperative, Competitive, or Individualistic? *Journal for the Education of the Gifted*, 16(1).

Maker, C.J. & Nielson, A.B. (1996) *Curriculum Development and Teaching Strategies for Gifted Learners*. 2nd ed. PRO-ED.

McCoach, D.B. & Siegle, D. (2003) Factors That Differentiate Underachieving Gifted Students From High-Achieving Gifted Students. *Gifted Child Quarterly*, 47(2), 144–154.

McCrady, B.S. & Ziedonis, D. (2001) American Psychiatric Association practice guideline for substance use disorders. *Behavior Therapy*, 32(2), 309-336.

McGrath, P. (2018). Education in Northern Ireland: Does it meet the needs of gifted students? *Gifted Education International* [online].

Meyers, L. (2014) Gifted Children: Not immune to low self-esteem. *Counseling Today* [online].

Mullis, I.V.S., Martin, M.O., Foy, P., Kelly, D.L., & Fishbein, B. (2020). *TIMSS 2019 International Results in Mathematics and Science*. TIMSS & PIRLS International Study Center [online].

NAGC (2005) *The History of Gifted and Talented Education*. National Association for Gifted Children [online].

National Association for Gifted Children (1988). *Frequently Asked Questions about Gifted Education* [online].

National Association for Gifted Children (2022) *Standard 2: Assessments* [online].

National Association for Gifted Children (2022) *Tests & Assessments* [online].

Neihart, M. (2011) *The Impact of Giftedness on Psychological Well-Being*. SENG [online].

Oak Crest Academy (2018) *11 Ways Gifted Students Learn Differently* [online]

Oak Crest Academy (2018) *Gifted Students Learn Differently in These 11 Ways* [online].

O'Mahoney, A. & Ryan, R.M.C. (2018) *SALF: Self-Assessment and Learning Folders*. Outside the Box Learning Resources.

O'Neal, E. (2017). *Got a gifted reader? Here are an educator's top tips for story time*. Pick Any Two [online].

O'Reilly, C. (2005) Maximising potential – both academic and social–emotional. In: Smith, C.M.M/ [ed.] *Including the Gifted and Talented: Making Inclusion Work for More Able and Gifted Learners*. Routledge.

Ozturk, M. & Debelak, C. (2008) Affective Benefits from Academic Competitions for Middle School Gifted Students. *Gifted Child Today* 31(2).

Porter, L. (2005) Young Gifted Children: Meeting Their Needs. Early Childhood Australia Research in Practice Series, 12 (3).

Porter, L. (2020). *Gifted Young Children: A guide for teachers and parents*. Routledge.

Post, G. (2016) *Who is the gifted underachiever? Four types of underachievement in gifted children*. Gifted Challenges [online].

Psychology Today (2022) Boredom. *Psychology Today* [online].

Reid, B.D. & McGuire, M.D. (1995). *Square pegs in round holes – These kids don't fit: High ability students with behavioral problems*. National Research Center on the Gifted and Talented.

Reis, S.M. & McCoach D.B. (2000) The underachievement of gifted students: What do we know and where do we go? *Gifted Child Quarterly*, 44, 152-170.

Reis, S.M., Neu, T.W. & McGuire, J.M. (1997). Case studies of high-ability students with learning disabilities who have achieved. *Exceptional Children*, 63(4), 463-479.

Renzulli, J. S. (2016) The three-ring conception of giftedness: A developmental model for promoting creative productivity. In: *Reflections on gifted education: Critical works by Joseph S. Renzulli and colleagues* (pp.55-90). Prufrock Press.

Rigsbee, C. (2018) *Strategies for Helping Stressed-Out Gifted Learners*. Teacher's Workshop [online].

Roeper, A. (2016) The Annemarie Roeper Method of Qualitative Assessment: My Journey. Roeper Review 38(4).

Rogers, K.B. (2002) *Re-forming Gifted Education: Matching the Program to the Child*. Great Potential Press.

Sahin, C. (Celik), & Schmidt, O. (2014) Teaching English Activities for the Gifted and Talented Students. *Journal for the Education of Gifted Young Scientists* 1(53).

Sakiey, E. (1980). *Reading for the Gifted: Instructional Strategies Based on Research*. ERIC [online].

Schapiro, M., Schneider, B.H., Shore, B.M. & Margison, J.A. (2009) Competitive Goal Orientations, Quality and Stability in Gifted and Other Adolescents' Friendships: A Test of Sullivan's Theory About the Harm Caused by Rivalry. *Gifted Child Quarterly*, 53(2) 71-88.

Schuler, P., Amend, E.R., Beaver-Gavin, K. & Beights, R. (2009) A Unique Challenge: Sorting Out the Differences between Giftedness and Asperger's Disorder. *Gifted Child Today*, 32(4), 57-63.

Schultz, J. (2022) *Social Anxiety in Kids: What You Need to Know*. Understood [online].

Seidenberg, M.S. (2013) The Science of Reading and Its Educational Implications. *Language Learning and Development*, 9(4), 331–360.

Seifert, D. (2016) *Top 5 Reasons why Vocabulary Matters*. InferCabulary [online].

Shade, R. (1991) Verbal Humor in Gifted Students and Students in the General Population: A Comparison of Spontaneous Mirth and Comprehension. *Journal for the Education of the Gifted*. 14(2).

Shenfield, T. (2016) How to Engage in Play With Your Children – and Enjoy It. *Advanced Psychology* [online].

Shenfield T. (2021) What is Creative Giftedness, and How Can Creativity be Nurtured in Gifted Children? *Advanced Psychology* [online].

Siegler, R.S. & Kotovsky, K. (1986) Two levels of giftedness: Shall ever the twain meet? In Sternberg, R.J. & Davidson, J.E. (Eds.) *Conceptions of giftedness*. Cambridge University Press.

Silverman, L.K. (2012). *Giftedness 101*. Springer Publishing Company.

Silverman, L.K., & Golon, A.S. (2008) Clinical Practice with Gifted Families. In Pfeiffer, S.I. (Ed.), *Handbook of Giftedness in Children: Psychoeducational Theory, Research, and Best Practices*. Springer.

Snyder, J. (2018) *Teaching Vocabulary to Gifted and Advanced Learners—Instructional Strategies that Work*. Soaring with Snyder [online].

Stanley, T. (2017) *How to spot a gifted child*. edCircuit [online].

Sternberg, R. J. (2005) WICS: A model of giftedness in leadership. *Roeper Review* 28(1) 37-44.

Stokes, B. (2004) *Stretch, Bend and Boggle: A week-by-week maths program for developing logic and problem-solving skills*. Hawker Brownlow Education.

Sutherland, M., and Stack, N. (2014) Ability as an additional support need: Scotland's inclusive approach to gifted education. *Centre for Educational Policy Studies Journal*, 4(3). 73-87.

Swanson, H. L. (1992). The relationship between metacognition and problem solving in gifted children. *Roeper Review*, 15(1), 43–48.

Taibbi, C. (2012) 'Bright Child' vs 'Gifted Learner': What's the Difference? *Psychology Today* [online].

TCEO (2008) *Student Diversity*. Tasmanian Catholic Education Office [online].

Thompson-Kroon, J.E. (2011) Defining Reality: The Parental Experience of Getting to a Diagnosis of Asperger Syndrome. PhD thesis, Gannon University.

Thompson, R.H., Cotnoir-Bichelman, N.M., McKerchar, P.M., Tate, T.L. & Dancho, K.A. (2013) Enhancing Early Communication through Infant Sign Training. *Journal of Applied Behaviour Analysis* 40(1).

Tirri, K. & Kuusisto, E. (2013) How Finland Serves Gifted and Talented Pupils. *Journal for the Education of the Gifted*, 36(1), 84-96.

Tolan, S.S. (1999). *Dabrowski's Over-excitabilities: A Layman's Explanation*. Hoagies' Gifted Education [online].

References

Tomlinson, C.A. (1997). The dos and don'ts of instruction: What it means to teach gifted learners well. *Instructional Leader*, 10(3), 1-3, 12.

Tomlinson, C.A. (1997) *What it Means to Teach Gifted Learners Well*. National Association for Gifted Children.

Tony, C. & Norah, F. (2009) *Special Educational Needs, Inclusion and Diversity*. McGraw-Hill

Udvari, S. J. & Schneider, B. H. (2000) Competition and the Adjustment of Gifted Children: A Matter of Motivation. *Roeper Review* 22(4) 212-216.

Vacca, J.A.L., Vacca, R.T. & Gove, M.K. (1991) *Instructor's Manual to Accompany Reading and Learning to Read*. HarperCollins.

Vahidi, S. (2015). *Major Turning Points in Gifted Education in the 20th Century*. Renzulli Center for Creativity, Gifted Education, and Talent Development [online].

VanTassel-Baska, J. (2006) A Content Analysis of Evaluation Findings Across 20 Gifted Programs: A Clarion Call for Enhanced Gifted Program Development. *Gifted Child Quarterly*, 50(3), 199-215.

Venosdale, K. (2011) *Google Plus: What does it mean for education?* Missouri State Teachers Association.

Vosslamber, A. (2002) Gifted Readers: Who Are They, and How Can They Be Served in the Classroom? *Gifted Child Today*, 25(2), 14-20.

Webb, J.T., Gore, J.L. & Amend, E.R. (2007) *A Parent's Guide to Gifted Children*. Great Potential Press.

Whitmore, J.R. (1985) *Characteristics of Intellectually Gifted Children*. 1985 Digest, Revised. ERIC Clearinghouse on Handicapped and Gifted Children, 1920 Association.

Wilson, H.E., & Adelson, J.L. (2018). Perfectionism: Helping Gifted Children Learn Healthy Strategies and Create Realistic Expectations. *Parenting for High Potential*, 7(3), 8.

Winner, E. (1996) *Gifted Children: Myths and Realities*. Basic Books.

www.openheartmeditation.com/

www.studyandcareers.ie/online-courses

ZeitgeistFilms (2020) Beyond the Visible: Hilma af Klint – official US trailer [online].

To keep up to date with the *How to Help* series, bookmark:

www.pavpub.com/howtohelp